Wordscapes

Barry Maybury

OXFORD UNIVERSITY PRESS

Oxford University Press, Ely House, London W.1

GLASGOW NEW YORK TORONTO MELBOURNE WELLINGTON
CAPE TOWN IBADAN NAIROBI DAR ES SALAAM LUSAKA
ADDIS ABABA BOMBAY CALCUTTA MADRAS KARACHI LAHORE DACCA
DELHI KUALA LUMPUR SINGAPORE HONG KONG TOKYO

By the same author:
Creative Writing for Juniors (B. T. Batsford Ltd. London)

First Published 1970
Reprinted 1972, 1974

Filmset by BAS Printers Ltd, Wallop, Hampshire
Printed in Great Britain by
Hazell Watson and Viney Ltd
Aylesbury, Bucks

Contents

Senses

Pushing and shoving

I stood there. The people's hats were blowing about. Pieces of paper were blown about, and trees were swaying about. Leaves of trees were falling. People were wearing coats with collars up, and the wind was blowing washing about. People's faces frown, and they look very cross. Clouds turn grey, and it starts to rain. People look even more cross, and umbrellas go up. They weren't up before, because the wind would turn them inside out. The smoke from chimneys blows the way the wind does, and it looks like fog in the sky. . . . A lady's scarf flaps in the wind, and grass sways this way and that. The wind does a lot of damage. At night it keeps people awake, because of the sound of dustbin lids, and milk bottles clanging, and being blown off. Buses blow on one side, and it makes you feel unsafe. If you go shopping people are blown about, and they fall into someone, and push them, and their parcels fall, and they start shouting at each other. Windows bang open and shut. This is all caused by the wind.

CAROL, aged 10

White is a dove
And lily of the valley
And a puddle of milk
Spilled in an alley—
A ship's sail
A kite's tail
A wedding veil
Hailstones and
Halibut bones
And some people's
Telephones.
The hottest and most blinding light
Is white.
And breath is white
When you blow it out on a frosty night.
White is the shining absence of all colour
Then absence is white
Out of touch
Out of sight.
White is marshmallow
And vanilla ice-cream
And the part you can't remember
In a dream.
White is the sound
Of a light foot walking
White is a pair of
Whispers talking.
White is the beautiful
Broken lace
Of snowflakes falling

7 On your face.
You can smell white
In a country room
Near the end of May
When the cherries bloom.

MARY O'NEILL

The term

A rumpled sheet
of brown paper
about the length

and apparent bulk
of a man was
rolling with the

wind slowly over
and over in
the street as

a car drove down
upon it and
crushed it to

the ground. Unlike
a man it rose
again rolling

with the wind over
and over to be as
it was before.

WILLIAM CARLOS WILLIAMS

In the playground

The leaves are rustling themselves in the trees and the trees are moving, groaning heavy sound. The twigs are crackling snapping and spluttering. They crackle and pop when you crunch them with your foot. The children scuffle and shuffle across the playground. They kick stones with a scrubbing sound. You can hear an engine in the lane whining whizzing down the bank. I can hear the children's voices talking. They sometimes make the birds twitter but the chattering birds have gone away today. It is winter. There is silence.

JOHN, aged 9

Beech leaves

In autumn down the beechwood path
  The leaves lie thick upon the ground.
It's there I love to kick my way
  And hear their crisp and crashing sound.

I am a giant, and my steps
  Echo and thunder to the sky.
How the small creatures of the woods
  Must quake and cower as I pass by!

This brave and merry noise I make
  In summer also when I stride
Down to the shining, pebbly sea
  And kick the frothing waves aside.

JAMES REEVES

Pleasant sounds

The rustling of leaves under the feet in woods and under hedges;
The crumpling of cat-ice and snow down wood-rides, narrow
    lanes, and every street causeway;
Rustling through a wood or rather rushing, while the wind halloos
    in the oak-top like thunder;
The rustle of birds' wings startled from their nests or flying unseen
    into the bushes;
The whizzing of larger birds overhead in a wood, such as crows,
    puddocks, buzzards;
The trample of robins and woodlarks on the brown leaves, and
    the patter of squirrels on the green moss;
The fall of an acorn on the ground, the pattering of nuts on the
    hazel branches as they fall from ripeness;
The flirt of the groundlark's wing from the stubbles—how sweet
    such pictures on dewy mornings, when the dew flashes from its
    brown feathers!

JOHN CLARE

Spring morning

There's the clip clop of horses on the sunhoneyed cobbles of the
humming streets, hammering of horseshoes, gobble quack and
cackle, tomtit twitter from the bird-ounced boughs, braying on
Donkey Down. Bread is baking, pigs are grunting, chop goes the
butcher, milk-churns bell, tills ring, sheep cough, dogs shout, saws
sing. Oh, the Spring whinny and morning moo from the clog
dancing farms, the gull's gab and rabble on the boat-bobbing
river and sea and the cockles bubbling in the sand, scamper of

sanderlings, curlew cry, crow caw, pigeon coo, clock strike, bull bellow, and the ragged gabble of the beargarden school as the women scratch and babble in Mrs Organ Morgan's general shop where everything is sold: custard, buckets, henna, rat-traps, shrimp-nets, sugar, stamps, confetti, paraffin, hatchets, whistles.

from *Under Milk Wood* by DYLAN THOMAS

Sink song

Scouring out the porridge pot,
   Round and round and round!

Out with all the scraith and scoopery.
Lift the eely ooly droopery,
Chase the glubbery slubbery gloopery
   Round and round and round!

Out with all the doleful dithery,
Ladle out the slimery slithery,
Hunt and catch the hithery thithery,
   Round and round and round!

Out with all the obbly gubbly,
On the stove it burns so bubbly,
Use the spoon and use it doubly,
   Round and round and round!

J. A. LINDON

Taste

You cut the lemon
The juice runs out.
Without any doubt
It's bitter, sour, watery
And sharp.
So sharp; it rings
It stings,
With bitterness.

There will be
A ting
As your mouth
Will ring, ring
Ring,
With a tang
And watery juice
Runs down your chin
Like a pin,
It tickles
And when it's finished
You think how bitter.

STEPHEN, aged 10

This is just to say

This is just to say
I have eaten
the plums
that were in
the icebox

and which
you were probably
saving
for breakfast

Forgive me
they were delicious
so sweet
and so cold

WILLIAM CARLOS WILLIAMS

A raw carrot

A raw carrot you get from the garden is scrumptious, munchious and delicious. You can break it off with a snap, and pop a bit in your mouth to crunch up and chew and when you chew it it tastes sweet and juicy, cold and crisp in your mouth. Then you hold it tight and bite into it with a terrific crack! You can feel great chunks of it being ground up by your teeth and every chew is mouthwatering and sweet. It is a rich and juicy thing a carrot is like free ice cream.

RAYMOND, aged 10

Hot cake

Winter has come; fierce is the cold;
In the sharp morning air new-risen we meet.
Rheum freezes in the nose;
Frost hangs about the chin.
For hollow bellies, for chattering teeth and shivering knees
What better than hot cake?
Soft as the down of spring,
Whiter than autumn floss!
Dense and swift the stream
Rises, swells and spreads.
Fragrance flies through the air,
Is scattered far and wide,
Steals down along the winds and wets
The covetous mouth of passer-by.
Servants and grooms
Throw sidelong glances, munch the empty air.
They lick their lips who serve;
While lines of envious lackeys by the wall
Stand dryly swallowing.

SHU HSI
translated by ARTHUR WALEY

A fat brown goose lay at one end of the table, and at the other end, on a bed of creased paper strewn with sprigs of parsley, lay a great ham, stripped of its outer skin and peppered over with crust crumbs, a neat paper frill round its shin, and beside this was a round of spiced beef. Between these rival ends ran parallel lines of side-dishes: two little minsters of jelly, red and yellow; a shallow dish full of blocks of blancmange and red jam, a large green leaf-shaped dish with a stalk-shaped handle, on which lay bunches of purple raisins and peeled almonds, a companion dish on which lay a solid rectangle of Smyrna figs, a dish of custard topped with grated nutmeg, a small bowl full of chocolates and sweets wrapped in gold and silver papers and a glass vase in which stood some tall celery stalks. In the centre of the table there stood, as sentries to a fruitstand which upheld a pyramid of oranges and American apples, two squat old-fashioned decanters of cut glass, one containing port and the other dark sherry. On the closed square piano a pudding in a huge yellow dish lay in waiting and behind it were three squads of bottles of stout and ale and minerals, drawn up according to the colours of their uniforms, the first two black, with brown and red labels, the third and smallest squad white, with transverse green sashes.

from *The Dead* by JAMES JOYCE

Seaside smells

I remember the smell of sea and seaweed, wet flesh, wet hair, wet bathing-dresses, the warm smell as of a rabbity field after rain, the smell of pop and splashed sunshades and toffee, the stable-and-straw smell of hot, tossed, tumbled, dung, and trodden sand, the swill-and-gaslamp smell of Saturday night, though the sun shone strong, from the bellying beer-tents, the smell of the vinegar on shelled cockles, winkle-smell, shrimp-smell, the dripping-oily backstreet winter-smell of chips in newspapers, the smell of ships from the sun-dazed docks round the corner of the sand-hills, the smell of the known and paddled-in sea . . .

from *Holiday Memory* by DYLAN THOMAS

House smells

Inside, there was a good smell of spicy cooking, jam-making, chintz, minced meat, musty books, coal fires, flowers—generally chrysanthemums—and mint imperials, which my Granny used to suck 'for her chest'. It was an utterly different smell to the one in our little flat in Cockburn Street, which was a compound of strong tobacco, wood shavings, boiled onions, floor polish and soot. I loved the sweet, old-maid smell of Granny's house, though I always felt that our own was the only right smell for a house to have. I was peculiarly sensitive to the smell of other people's houses. My Granny Johnson's smelt of snuff and shaving soap and boot polish and Woodbines. Mrs Battey's smelt of washing and hot girdle scones. But most of the houses in our street had the unmistakable, unforgettable smell of poverty—an airless, stuffy, rancid smell, as if the very air, like the tea-leaves, had been used over and over again. It was a stale and sour smell of cold, unwashed sheets and bodies, the greasy aroma of pans of vegetable broth, the mustiness of dry crusts, the breath children exhale when they chew dry bread—the very essence of misery.

from *The Only Child* by JAMES KIRKUP

Smells

Why is it that the poets tell
So little of the sense of smell?
These are the odours I love well:

The smell of coffee, freshly ground;
Or rich plum pudding, holly-crowned;
Or onions fried and deeply browned.

The fragrance of a fumy pipe;
The smell of apples, newly ripe;
And printers' ink on leaden type.

Woods by moonlight in September
Breathe most sweet; and I remember
Many a smoky camp-fire ember.

Camphor, turpentine, and tea,
The balsam of a Christmas tree,
These are the whiffs of gramarye—
A ship smells best of all to me!

CHRISTOPHER MORLEY

Blackberry-picking

Late August, given heavy rain and sun
For a full week, the blackberries would ripen.
At first, just one, a glossy purple clot
Among others, red, green, hard as a knot.
You ate that first one and its flesh was sweet
Like thickened wine: summer's blood was in it
Leaving stains upon the tongue and lust for
Picking. Then red ones inked up and that hunger
Sent us out with milk-cans, pea-tins, jam-pots
Where briars scratched and wet grass bleached our boots.
Round hayfields, cornfields and potato-drills
We trekked and picked until the cans were full,
Until the tinkling bottom had been covered
With green ones, and on top big dark blobs burned
Like a plate of eyes. Our hands were peppered
With thorn pricks, our palms sticky as Bluebeard's.

We hoarded the fresh berries in the byre.
But when the bath was filled we found a fur,
A rat-grey fungus, glutting on our cache.
The juice was stinking too. Once off the bush
The fruit fermented, the sweet flesh would turn sour.
I always felt like crying. It wasn't fair
That all the lovely canfuls smelt of rot.
Each year I hoped they'd keep, knew they would not.

SEAMUS HEANEY

At first it was deafening. You couldn't hear a thing if anybody spoke to you. There were black oily machines everywhere spinning their drills like silver needles churning out the blue metal in long winding coils all over the floor which was like thick black mud. You had to mind you didn't slip. A bit further down there were some men welding with masks on like men from outer space. They had torches shooting blue flames which you could not look at because they might blind you. There was a terribly choking smell coming from these welding torches and I could taste it in my mouth a long time after we got back to school. Every time a man finished a job he threw a piece of metal into an iron box and this made a deafening clang! We only stayed in there a few minutes and we were not allowed to go close but it was enough for me. I never want to go there again.

GAIL, aged 10

Weather and Seasons

Hard frost

Frost called to water 'Halt!'
And crusted the moist snow with sparkling salt;
Brooks, their own bridges, stop,
And icicles in long stalactites drop,
And tench in water-holes
Lurk under gluey glass like fish in bowls.

In the hard-rutted lane
At every footstep breaks a brittle pane,
And tinkling trees ice-bound,
Changed into weeping willows, sweep the ground;
Dead boughs take root in ponds
And ferns on windows shoot their ghostly fronds.

But vainly the fierce frost
Interns poor fish, ranks trees in an armed host,
Hangs daggers from house-eaves
And on the windows ferny ambush weaves;
In the long war grown warmer
The sun will strike him dead and strip his armour.

ANDREW YOUNG

Icicles

Hanging from the porch
Are slippery white icicles.
Gone the sun's scorch,
Now the frosts bite.

They hang there pointed and long,
Now, only now that summer has gone.
Transparent and cold, over the porch they hang low,
Through ice and cold winds,
Through winter and snow.

Softly, white icicles float from the sky,
Cold and hard hang icicles,
White with silver sheen,
Now the winter has come and warm summer has been.

                                        Boy, aged 11

Snow

I am white
And I fall from a hedge
I cover the ground
And don't make a sound.

                                        Boy, aged 8

Snow

White bird featherless
Flew from Paradise,
Pitched on the castle wall;
Along came Lord Landless
Took it up handless,
And rode away horseless to the King's white hall.

Anon.

Every branch big with it,
Bent every twig with it;
Every fork like a white web-foot;
Every street and pavement mute:
Some flakes have lost their way, and grope back upward, when
Meeting those meandering down they turn and descend again.
The palings are glued together like a wall,
And there is no waft of wind with the fleecy fall.

A sparrow enters the tree,
Whereon immediately
A snow-lump thrice his own slight size
Descends on him and showers his head and eyes,
And overturns him,
And near inurns him,
And lights on a nether twig, when its brush
Starts off a volley of other lodging lumps with a rush.

The steps are a blanched slope,
Up which, with feeble hope,
A black cat comes, wide-eyed and thin;
And we take him in.

THOMAS HARDY

In midwinter a wood was . . .

In midwinter a wood was
where the sand-coloured deer ran
through quietness.
It was a marvellous thing
to see those deer running.

Softer than ashes
snow lay all winter where they ran,
and in the wood a holly tree was.
God, it was a marvellous thing
to see the deer running.

Between lime trunks grey or green
branch-headed stags went by
silently trotting.
A holly tree dark and crimson
sprouted at the wood's centre, thick and high
without a whisper, no other berry so fine.

Outside the wood was black midwinter,
over the downs that reared so solemn
wind rushed in gales, and strong here
wrapped around wood and holly fire
(where deer among the close limes ran)
with a storming circle of its thunder.
Under the trees it was a marvellous thing
To see the deer running.

PETER LEVI

Winter days

Biting air
Winds blow
City streets
Under snow

Noses red
Lips sore
Runny eyes
Hands raw

Chimneys smoke
Cars crawl
Piled snow
On garden wall

Slush in gutters
Ice in lanes
Frosty patterns
On window panes

Morning call
Lift up head
Nipped by winter
Stay in bed

GARETH OWEN

Winter

Snow wind-whipt to ice
    Under a hard sun:
Stream-runnels curled hoar
    Crackle, cannot run.

29 Robin stark dead on twig,
       Song stiffened in it:
    Fluffed feathers may not warm
       Bone-thin linnet:

    Big-eyed rabbit, lost,
       Scrabbles the snow,
    Searching for long-dead grass
       With frost-bit toe:

    Mad-tired on the road
       Old Kelly goes;
    Through crookt fingers snuffs the air
       Knife-cold in his nose.

    Hunger-weak, snow-dazzled,
       Old Thomas Kelly
    Thrusts his hands, for warmth,
       'Twixt waistcoat and belly.

                                   RICHARD HUGHES

Spring

Nothing is so beautiful as spring—
       When weeds, in wheels, shoot long and lovely and lush;
       Thrush's eggs look little low heavens, and thrush
Through the echoing timber does so rinse and wring
The ear, it strikes like lightnings to hear him sing;
       The glassy peartree leaves and blooms, they brush
       The descending blue; that blue is all in a rush
With richness; the racing lambs too have fair their fling.

                       From *Spring* by GERARD MANLEY HOPKINS

in Just-
spring   when the world is mud-
lucious the little
lame balloonman

whistles   far   and wee

and eddieandbill come
running from marbles and
piracies and it's
spring

when the world is puddle-wonderful

the queer
old balloonman whistles
far   and   wee
and bettyandisbel come dancing

from hop-scotch and jump-rope and

it's
spring
and

    the

       goat-footed

balloonMan   whistles
far
and
wee

                                         e. e. cummings

In a cornfield

A silence of full noontide heat
Grew on them at their toil:
The farmer's dog woke up from sleep,
The green snake hid her coil
Where grass grew thickest; bird and beast
Sought shadows as they could,
The reaping men and women paused
And sat down where they stood;
They ate and drank and were refreshed,
For rest from toil is good.

CHRISTINA ROSSETTI

We sat by the roadside and scooped the dust with our hands and made little piles in the gutters. Then we slid through the grass and lay on our backs and just stared at the empty sky. There was nothing to do. Nothing moved or happened, nothing happened at all except summer. Small heated winds blew over our faces, dandelion seeds floated by, burnt sap and roast nettles tingled our nostrils together with the dull rust smell of dry ground. The grass was June high and had come up with a rush, a massed entanglement of species, crested with flowers and spears of wild wheat, and coiled with clambering vetches, the whole if it humming with blundering bees and flickering with scarlet butterflies. Chewing grass on our backs, the grass scaffolding the sky, the summer was all we heard; cuckoos crossed distances on chains of cries, flies buzzed and choked in the ears, and the saw-toothed chatter of mowing machines drifted on waves of air from the fields.

We moved. We went to the shop and bought sherbet and sucked it through sticks of liquorice. Sucked gently, the sherbet merely dusted the tongue; too hard, and you choked with sweet powders; or if you blew back through the tube the sherbet bag burst and you disappeared in a blizzard of sugar. Sucking and blowing, coughing and weeping, we scuffled our way down the lane.

from *Cider with Rosie* by LAURIE LEE

33 Hot day

The sunny slow lulling afternoon yawns and moons through the dozy town. The sea lolls, laps and idles in, with fishes sleeping in its lap. The meadows still as Sunday, the shut-eye tasselled bulls, the goat-and-daisy dingles, nap happy and lazy. The dumb duckponds snooze. Clouds sag and pillow on Llaregyb Hill. Pigs grunt in a wet wallow-bath, and smile as they snort and dream. They dream of the acorned swill of the world, the rooting for pig-fruit, the bagpipe dugs of the mother sow, the squeal and snuffle of yesses of the women pigs in rut. They mud-bask and snout in the pig-loving sun; their tails curl; they rollick and slobber and snore to deep, smug, after-swill sleep. Donkeys angelically drowse on Donkey Down.

from *Under Milk Wood* by DYLAN THOMAS

Autumn

Yellow the bracken,
Golden the sheaves,
Rosy the apples,
Crimson the leaves;
Mist on the hillside,
Clouds grey and white.
Autumn good morning!
Winter, good night!

FLORENCE HOATSON

Whirling leaves, golden and brown,
Twisting and turning,
Hurrying down.

Driving wind, gusty and strong,
Whistling and sighing,
Rushing along.

Scudding clouds, grey-leaden sky,
Laughing and playing,
Galloping by.

Roaming birds, gathered for flight,
Chirping and preening,
Seeking sunlight.

Curling smoke, mindful of fires,
Blowing and puffing,
Hiding the spires.

Drooping rose, scatter to earth,
Dying and fading,
Waiting new birth.

F. POLITZER

Fog

London . . . November weather. As much mud in the streets as if the waters had but newly retired from the face of the earth . . . Smoke lowering down from chimney-pots, making a soft black drizzle, with flakes of soot in it as big as full-grown snowflakes— gone into mourning, one might imagine, for the death of the sun. Dogs, undistinguishable in mire. Horses, scarcely better; splashed to their very blinkers. Foot passengers, jostling one another's umbrellas, in a gerneral infection of ill-temper, and losing their foot-hold at street-corners, where tens of thousands of other foot passengers have been slipping and sliding since the day broke (if this day ever broke), adding new deposits to the crust upon crust of mud . . .

Fog everywhere. Fog up the river, where it flows among green aits and meadows; fog down the river, where it rolls defiled among the tiers of shipping . . . Fog on the Essex marshes. Fog on the Kentish heights. Fog creeping into the cabooses of collier-brigs; fog lying out in the yards, and hovering in the rigging of great ships; fog drooping on the gunwales of barges and small boats. Fog in the eyes and throats of ancient Greenwich pensioners, wheezing by the fireside in their wards; fog in the stem and bowl of the afternoon pipe of the wrathful skipper, down in his close cabin, fog cruelly pinching the toes and fingers of his shivering little 'prentice boy on the deck. Chance people on the bridges peeping over the parapets into a lower sky of fog, with fog all round them, as if they were up in a balloon, and hanging in the misty clouds.

from *Bleak House* by CHARLES DICKENS

Fog

The fog comes
on little cat feet.
It sits looking
over harbour and city
on silent haunches
and then moves on.

CARL SANDBURG

Rain

See the rain in the streets,
See the people rushing for shelter,
Pools of water on the path,
Rippling in the drains.
If very bad it thunders and lightens.
If in the house it goes pitter-patter.
Everybody is wearing macs and wellingtons;
See the dripping umbrellas. . . .
On all the buildings, steamed-up windows.
If out too long you catch a chill.
It goes dark and dreary.
Sometimes your wallpaper is damp.
See the damp clothes round the fire.
And, rushing the washing in,
See your reflection in the pools.

IRENE, aged 11

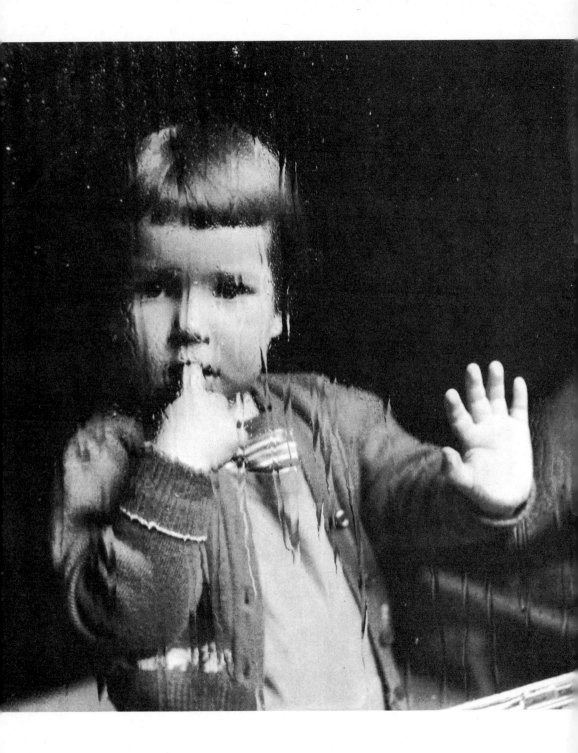

Storm

Now it is almost night, from the bronzey soft sky
jugfull after jugfull of pure white liquid fire, bright white
tipples over and spills down,
and is gone
and gold-bronze flutters beat through the thick upper air.
And as the electric liquid pours out, sometimes
a still brighter white snake wriggles among it, spilled
and tumbling wriggling down the sky:
and then the heavens crackle with uncouth sounds.

from *Storm in the Black Forest* by D. H. LAWRENCE

After rain

The rain of a night and a day and a night
Stops at the light
Of this pale choked day. The peering sun
Sees what has been done.
The road under the trees had a border new
Of purple hue
Inside the border of bright thin grass:
For all that has
Been left by November of leaves is torn
From hazel and thorn
And the greater trees. Throughout the copse
No dead leaf drops
On grey grass, green moss, burnt-orange fern,
At the wind's return:
The leaflets out of the ash-tree shed
Are thinly spread
In the road, like little black fish, inlaid,
As if they played.
What hangs from the myriad branches down there
So hard and bare
Is twelve yellow apples lovely to see
On one crab-tree.
And on each twig of every tree in the dell
Uncountable
Crystals both dark and bright of the rain
That begins again.

EDWARD THOMAS

Pearls on the grass

After the beautiful rain,
The rocks shine under the sun,
Like the droplets on the cobweb
Amongst the green, green grass.

GEETA MOHANTY, aged 13

Storm at sea

Sometimes I plunge through the press of the waves
Unexpectedly, delving to the earth,
The ocean bed. The waters ferment,
Sea-horses foaming.
The whale-mere roars, fiercely rages,
Waves beat upon the shore; stones and sand,
Seaweed and saltspray, are savagely flung
Against the dunes when, wrestling
Far beneath the waves, I disturb the earth,
The vast depths of the sea. Nor can I escape
My ocean bed before he permits me who is my pilot
On every journey. Tell me, wise man:
Who separates me from the sea's embrace,
When the waters become quiet once more,
The waves calm which before had covered me?

Anglo-Saxon riddle
Translated by KEVIN CROSSLEY-HOLLAND

And it was windy weather

Now the winds are riding by;
Clouds are galloping the sky;

Bush and tree are lashing bare,
Savage boughs on savage air;

Crying, as they lash and sway,
—Pull the roots out of the clay!

Lift away: away:
Away!

Leave security, and speed
From the root, the mud, the mead!

Into sea and air, we go!
To chase the gull, the moon!—and know,

—Flying high!
Flying high!—

All the freedom of the sky!
All the freedom of the sky!

JAMES STEPHENS

A Windy Day

This wind brings all dead things to life,
Branches that lash the air like whips
And dead leaves rolling in a hurry
Or peering in a rabbit's burry
Or trying to push down a tree;
Gates that fly open to the wind
And close again behind,
The fields that are a flowing sea
And make the cattle look like ships;
Straws glistening and stiff
Lying on air as on a shelf
And the pond that leaps to leave itself;
And feathers too that rise and float,
Each feather changed into a bird,
And line-hung sheets that crack and strain;
Even the sun-greened coat,
That through so many winds has served,
The scarecrow struggles to put on again.

ANDREW YOUNG

Creatures

Worms and the wind

Worms would rather be worms.
Ask a worm and he says, 'Who knows what a worm knows?'
Worms go down and up and over and under.
Worms like tunnels.
When worms talk they talk about the worm world.
Worms like it in the dark.
Neither the sun nor the moon interests a worm.
Zigzag worms hate circle worms.
Curve worms never trust square worms.
Worms know what worms want.
Slide worms are suspicious of crawl worms.
One worm asks another, 'How does your belly drag today?'
The shape of a crooked worm satisfies a crooked worm.
A straight worm says, 'Why not be straight?'
Worms tired of crawling begin to slither.
Long worms slither farther than short worms.
Middle-sized worms say, 'It is nice to be neither long nor short.'
Old worms teach young worms to say, 'Don't be sorry for me unless
   you have been a worm and lived in worm places and read worm
   books.'
When worms go to war they dig in, come out and fight, dig in
   again, come out and fight again, dig in again, and so on.
Worms underground never hear the wind overground and some-
   times they ask, 'What is this wind we hear of?'

CARL SANDBURG

Beetle

A beetle caught my eye, one day,
　　Beside the path;
There, with his head buried deep in a daisy-centre,
Pigging and bolting it—great, scented, yellow mouthfuls—
　　With the space he had already eaten
　　Blackened around him;
There he gorged, standing on his ridiculous, gluttonous head,
　　With his hard, thin legs
　　Straight up in the forgotten air,
And his head deep in a dim, succulent heaven.

HUGH FINN

The garden snail

This backyard
　　cousin
　　　　to the octopus
Sees
　　through two filmy
　　　　stems
On his head, at
　　need
　　　　can peer round
　Corners, and
　　so betrays his

45   huge
    Timidity. He
        moves on his
            single
    Elastic foot
        seldom,
            preferring
    Anonymity
        to danger,
            seems
    Often to be
        meditating
            a very tough
    Problem, likes
        green leaves
            and water.
    Shyness
        is his prime
            virtue.
    Though I have seen
        one,
            on a blue day
    In summer,
        go climbing
            all afternoon
    With his brown shell
        up the wobbly tall
            grass,
    For a good
        look-round
            at the wide world.

ROBERT WALLACE

Tortoise

Lumbering carefully over stone and earth,
   Edging, stumbling, groping blindly,
To the favourite place of Michaelmas daisies.
   His food finished, now the tortoise
Feels his way one foot after another,
   Choosing a path among the grass,
Which looks like willows hovering high above his hard shell.
   Afternoon appears, sleep overpowers the beast.
Making heavy footsteps the tortoise finds a sleeping-place,
   One eye closes and the scum of the eyelid passes over both eyes,
The tortoise falls into a shelled sleep.
   Dawn; and he trundles off to find food,
He claws his way over the rockery,
   Which appears to him to be like the Andes,
Passing through glades of raspberries;
   And at last he finds his food,
Lettuce!
   Clumsily he opens his leather-hard jaws,
Draws his fire-red tongue out,
   Then, with a churning of cranking and creaking efforts,
He closes his mouth upon the lettuce;
   Tortoise now returns and digs with great speed,
To hide himself from winter.
   The hole dug, he retreats in his creaking wet-covered shell,
To sleep.

DAVID SPEECHLEY

To a squirrel at Kyle-na-no

Come play with me;
Why should you run
Through the shaking tree
As though I'd a gun
To strike you dead?
When all I would do
Is to scratch your head
And let you go.

W. B. YEATS

My dog Sam

My dog Sam is a mongrel, a one-eyed terror is he. They call him
a mischievous beggar because he will fight anybody. He fights
other dogs who are too big for him, he fights cats and chases them
up trees and people throw buckets over him but he does not care
because he has a thick skin. He just goes off somewhere and finds
a bone he has buried and lies about in a hedge. He has lots of fun
because he likes adventure. He is supposed to be white with black
markings on him but he's usually not very clean when he comes
home, he plays too much to keep clean. When I wash him he
comes up lovely and his coat is white and wiry and tough. He lost
his eye in a motor car accident once when he was run over. I
thought he was dead and had to be put to sleep but it just knocked
him about a bit and glazed his eye and the vet said he wouldn't
be able to see out of it very well again. I was very unhappy at
the time but he doesn't seem to care very much so I got over it.
The one-eyed wonder we call him now. He doesn't mind, he knows
we're only joking and he has a lot of fun in him. He can take a
joke. He's a tough dog, and we have some good times.

BARBARA, aged 10

Now from the woods

Now from the woods, mistrustful and sharp-eyed
The fox in silent darkness seems to glide,
Stealing around us, listening as he goes,
If chance the cock or stammering capon crows,
Or goose, or nodding duck, should darkling cry,
As if apprised of lurking danger nigh.

ROBERT BLOOMFIELD

The eagle

He clasps the crag with crooked hands;
Close to the sun in lonely lands,
Ring'd with the azure world, he stands.

The wrinkled sea beneath him crawls;
He watches from his mountain walls,
And like a thunderbolt he falls.

ALFRED, LORD TENNYSON

An otter

Underwater eyes, an eel's
Oil of water body, neither fish nor beast is the otter:
Four-legged yet water-gifted, to outfish fish;
With webbed feet and long ruddering tail
And a round head like an old tomcat.

Brings the legend of himself
From before wars or burials, in spite of hounds and vermin—
poles;
Does not take root like the badger. Wanders, cries;
Gallops along land he no longer belongs to;
Re-enters the water by melting.

from *An Otter* by TED HUGHES

Wild horse

With shiny skin
  And fiercest eye
Clattering hoof
  Will never die.

From memory of mine
  The horse (if wild)
A creature fine
  Who's always bright

Yet man took horse
  To call his own
And broke him in
  With reins and such.

Man used a whip
  'Twas very coarse
And took the life
  From wild horse

That proud creature
  Jumping free!
Is now a sad and gloomy one
  Oh, think! of what the man has done

Wild, free
  Full of glee
That was
  The wild one!

53   Shame on man
        To do what's done
    Took spirit, soul, all joy as well
        Oh—! wild horse!

HILLARY ALLEN, aged 9

Snake

I saw a young snake glide
Out of the mottled shade
And hang, limp on a stone:
A thin mouth, and a tongue
Stayed, in the still air.

It turned; it drew away;
Its shadow bent in half;
It quickened, and was gone.

I felt my slow blood warm.
I longed to be that thing,
The pure, sensuous form.

And I may be, some time.

THEODORE ROETHKE

Snakes

. . . we arrived at the edge of the pit, and in the lamplight it looked to me nothing more nor less than an extremely large grave. My friend's description of it had been accurate enough, but what he had failed to tell me was that the sides of the pit consisted of dry, crumbling earth, honeycombed with cracks and holes that offered plenty of hiding-places for any number of snakes. While I crouched down on the edge of the pit, the lamp was solemnly lowered into the depths so that I might spy out the land and try to identify the snakes. Up to that moment I had cheered myself with the thought that, after all, the snakes might turn out to be a harmless variety, but when the light reached the bottom this hope was shattered, for I saw that the pit was simply crawling with young Gaboon vipers, one of the most deadly snakes in the world.

During the daytime these snakes are very sluggish and it is quite a simple job to capture them, but at night, when they wake up and hunt for their food, they can be unpleasantly quick. These young ones in the pit were each about two feet long and a couple of inches in diameter, and they were all, as far as I could judge, very much awake. They wriggled round and round the pit with great rapidity, and kept lifting their heavy, arrow-shaped heads and contemplating the lamp, flicking their tongues out and in in a most suggestive manner.

from *Encounters With Animals* by GERALD DURRELL

India

They hunt, the velvet tigers in the jungle,
The spotted jungle full of shapeless patches—
Sometimes they're leaves, sometimes they're hanging flowers,
Sometimes they're hot gold patches of the sun:
They hunt, the velvet tigers in the jungle!

What do they hunt by glimmering pools of water,
By the round silver Moon, the Pool of Heaven—
In the striped grass, amid the barkless trees—
The stars scattered like eyes of beasts above them!

What do they hunt, their hot breath scorching insects,
Insects that blunder blindly in the way,
Vividly fluttering—they also are hunting,
Are glittering with a tiny ecstasy!

The grass is flaming and the trees are growing,
The very mud is gurgling in the pools,
Green toads are watching, crimson parrots flying,
Two pairs of eyes meet one another glowing—
They hunt, the velvet tigers in the jungle.

                                        W. J. Turner

Dolphins in blue water

Hey! Crackerjack—jump!
Blue water,
Pink water,
Swirl, flick, flitter;
Snout into a wave-trough,
Plunge, curl.
Bow over,
Under,
Razor-cut and tumble.
Roll, turn—
Straight—and shoot at the sky,
All rose-flame drippings.
Down ring,
Drop,
Nose under,
Hoop,
Tail,
Dive,
And gone;
With smooth over-swirlings of blue water,
Oil-smooth cobalt,
Slipping, liquid lapis lazuli,
Emerald shadings,
Tintings of pink and ochre.
Prismatic slidings
Underneath a windy sky.

AMY LOWELL

Fish

A fish dripping
sparkling drops
of crystal water,
pulled from the lake;
long has it dwelt
in the cool water,
in the cold water
of the lake.

Long has it wandered
to and fro
over the bottom
of the lake
among mysterious
recesses
there in the semi-
light of the water;

Now to appear
surprised, aghast,
out of its element
into the day;
out of the cold
and shining lake
the fish dripping
sparkling water.

W. W. E. Ross

Our local zoo

Expert officials at our Zoo
From long research at Timbuctoo
Conclude our winter's much too keen
For creatures of the tropic scene
And have provided woollen pants
For giraffes and elephants,
Vests for the chimpanzees, and bloomers
To fit the more fastiduous pumas.
Loud is the crowd in cachinnation
At this fantastic innovation,
And yet not more fantastic is it
Than many folk who pay their visit
In garbs of immemorial habit
In furs of fox and stoat and rabbit,
In leopard pantaloons *et al.*,
Peculiar to the animal,
And never feel uncertainty
Which side the bars they ought to be.

GEOFFREY JOHNSON

His first flight

The young seagull was alone on his ledge. His two brothers and his sister had already flown away the day before. He had been afraid to fly with them. Somehow when he had taken a little run forward to the brink of the ledge and attempted to flap his wings he became afraid. The great expanse of sea stretched down beneath, and it was such a long way down—miles down. He felt certain that his wings would never support him, so he bent his head and ran away back to the little hole under the ledge where he slept at night. Even when each of his brothers and his little sister, whose wings were far shorter than his own, ran to the brink, flapped their wings, and flew away he failed to muster up courage to take that plunge which appeared to him so desperate. His father and mother had come around calling to him shrilly, up-braiding him, threatening to let him starve on his ledge unless he flew away. But for the life of him he could not move.

That was twenty-four hours ago. Since then nobody had come near him. The day before, all day long, he had watched his parents flying about with his brothers and sisters, perfecting them in the art of flight, teaching them how to skim the waves and how to dive for fish. He had, in fact, seen his older brother catch his first herring and devour it, standing on a rock, while his parents circled around raising a proud cackle. And all the morning the whole family had walked about on the big plateau midway down the opposite cliff, taunting him with his cowardice.

The sun was now ascending the sky, blazing warmly on his ledge that faced the south. He felt the heat because he had not eaten since the previous nightfall. Then he had found a dried piece of mackerel's tail at the far end of his ledge. Now there was not a single scrap of food left. He had searched every inch, rooting among the rough, dirt-caked straw nest where he and his brothers and sister had been hatched. He even gnawed at the dried pieces of spotted eggshell. It was like eating part of himself. He had then trotted back and forth from one end of the ledge to the other, his grey body the colour of the cliff, his long grey legs stepping daintily, trying to find some means of reaching his parents with-out having to fly. But on each side of him the ledge ended in a sheer fall of precipice, with the sea beneath. And between him and his parents there was a deep wide chasm. Surely he could reach them without flying if he could only move northwards along the cliff face? But then on what could he walk? There was no ledge, and he was not a fly. And above him he could see nothing. The precipice was sheer, and the top of it was perhaps farther away than the sea beneath him.

He stepped slowly out to the brink of the ledge, and, standing on one leg with the other leg hidden under his wing, he closed one eye, then the other, and pretended to be falling asleep. Still they took no notice of him. He saw his two brothers and his sister lying on the plateau dozing, with their heads sunk into their necks. His father was preening the feathers on his white back. Only his mother was looking at him. She was standing on a little high hump on the plateau, her white breast thrust forward. Now and again she tore at a piece of fish that lay at her feet, and then scraped each side of her beak on the rock. The sight of the food maddened him. How he loved to tear food that way, scraping his beak now and again to whet it! He uttered a low cackle. His mother cackled too, and looked over at him.

'Ga, ga, ga,' he cried, begging her to bring him over some food. 'Gaw-ool-ah,' she screamed back derisively. But he kept calling plaintively, and after a minute or so he uttered a joyful scream. His mother had picked up a piece of fish and was flying across to him with it. He leaned out eagerly, tapping the rock with his feet, trying to get nearer to her as she flew across. But when she was just opposite him, abreast of the ledge, she halted, her legs hanging limp, her wings motionless, the piece of fish in her beak almost within reach of his beak. He waited a moment in surprise, wondering why she did not come nearer, and then, maddened by hunger, he dived at the fish. With a loud scream he fell outwards and downwards into space. His mother had swooped upwards. As he passed beneath her he heard the swish of her wings. Then a monstrous terror siezed him and his heart stood still. He could hear nothing. But it only lasted a moment. The next moment he felt his wings spread outwards. The wind rushed against his breast feathers, then under his stomach and against his wings. He could feel the tips of his wings cutting the air. He was not falling headlong now. He was soaring gradually downwards and outwards. He was no longer afraid. He just felt a bit dizzy. Then he flapped his wings once and he soared upwards. He uttered a joyous scream and flapped them again. He soared higher. He raised his breast and banked against the wind. 'Ga, ga, ga. Ga, ga, ga. Gaw-ool-ah.' His mother swooped past him, her wings making a loud noise. He answered her with another scream. Then his father flew over him screaming. Then he saw his two brothers and his sister flying around him curveting and banking and soaring and diving.

Then he completely forgot that he had not always been able to fly, and commenced himself to dive and soar and curvet, shrieking shrilly.

He was near the sea now, flying straight over it, facing straight out over the ocean. He saw a vast green sea beneath him, with little ridges moving over it, and he turned his beak sideways and crowed amusedly. His parents and his brothers and sister had landed on this green floor in front of him. They were beckoning to him, calling shrilly. He dropped his legs to stand on the green sea. His legs sank into it. He screamed with fright and attempted to rise again, flapping his wings. But he was tired and weak with hunger and he could not rise, exhausted by the strange exercise. His feet sank into the green sea, and then his belly touched it and he sank no farther. He was floating on it. And around him his family was screaming, praising him, and their beaks were offering him scraps of dog-fish.

He had made his first flight.

LIAM O'FLAHERTY

Our estate

Just remembered, suppose I ought to tell you something about where we used to live. Well you know these big housing estates, well it was one of them. They were right wide streets with like big grass verges and that. We'd only lived there since just before I was born. It was all new, and even now they were still building bits on to it all over the shop. Down at the bottom of Parkside there were some new houses that no one had moved into yet. We used to go down there on Saturday afternoons. There were splashes all over the walls where we'd been throwing mud-balls, and all the fences had footmarks where all the kids from the Catholic school had been seeing how high up they could kick.

It was like that all over the estate. There were big like greens all over with these little fences round, only most of the fences had been pulled up when we went chumping for bonfire night, and these greens had all paths worn across them where people had been taking short cuts.

from *There is a Happy Land* by KEITH WATERHOUSE

Our back street

From the old blackening shop hung a torn, dirty advertisement, limp and wet after a shower of rain. Mingled shouts from children playing ball come echoing down the street as they play round the old gas-lamp. Two women were standing at the gate of their neighbour bragging about their new coat or pair of shoes or talking about their families or the doings of their neighbours. Most of the children usually crowded round the old lamp-post at the end of the street playing or talking about television. It is a dirty but merry street and no proper road only coke and dirt. Black soot is caked to the bricks and wispy smoke comes from the square chimney pots. The grumpy old men wearily sit down in the scraggy gardens talking of their younger days. The dustbins were in an awful condition but nobody cared. The street was never empty.

Girl, aged 10

It was a long time ago

I'll tell you, shall I, something I remember?
Something that still means a great deal to me.
It was long ago.

A dusty road in summer I remember.
A mountain, and an old house, and a tree
That stood, you know,

Behind the house. An old woman I remember
In a red shawl with a grey cat on her knee
Humming under a tree.

She seemed the oldest thing I can remember,
But then perhaps I was not more than three.
It was a long time ago.

I dragged on the dusty road, and I remember
How the old woman looked over the fence at me
And seemed to know

How it felt to be three, and called out, I remember
'Do you like bilberries and cream for tea?'
I went under the tree

And while she hummed, and the cat purred, I remember
How she filled a saucer with berries and cream for me
So long ago,

Such berries and such cream as I remember
I never had seen before and never see
Today, you know.

69   And that is almost all I can remember,
The house, the mountain, the grey cat on her knee,
Her red shawl, and the tree,

And the taste of the berries, the feel of the sun I remember,
And the smell of everything that used to be
So long ago,

Till the heat on the road outside again I remember,
And how the long dusty road seemed to have for me
No end, you know.

That is the farthest thing I can remember.
It won't mean much to you. It does to me.
Then I grew up, you see.

ELEANOR FARJEON

Tall nettles

Tall nettles cover up, as they have done
These many springs, the rusty harrow, the plough
Long worn out, and the roller made of stone:
Only the elm butt tops the nettles now.

This corner of the farmyard I like most:
As well as any bloom upon a flower
I like the dust on the nettles, never lost
Except to prove the sweetness of a shower.

EDWARD THOMAS

An abandoned church

Roofless and eyeless, weed-sodden, dank, old, cold—
Fickly the sunset glimmered through the rain,
Gilded the gravestones—faded out again;
A storm-cock shrilled its aeon-old refrain,
    Lambs bleated from their fold.

WALTER DE LA MARE

The railway station

Trains coming in,
Trains going out,
Buzzing, screeching,
Grinding, scraping.

Whizzing past you,
Not caring for you,
Whistles whistling,
Brakes screeching.

People running,
People walking,
Shuffling, scuffling,
Along the wide crowded platform.

People get on the trains,
Opening and shutting doors,
The platform is almost deserted,
People no longer exist there.

GWYNETH, aged 11

I go to Weld Park Primary,
It's near the Underpass
And five blocks past the Cemetery
And two roads past the Gas
Works with the big tower that smells so bad
    me and me mates put our hankies over our
       faces and pretend we're being attacked
          by poison gas . . . and that.

There's this playground with lines for rounders,
And cricket stumps chalked on the wall,
And kids with their coats for goalposts
Booting a tennis ball
Around all over the place and shoutin' and arguin'
    about offside and they always kick it over
       the garden wall next door and she
         goes potty and tells our head teacher
         and he gets right ratty with
           everybody and stops us playin'
            football . . .
              . . . and everything.

We have this rule at our school
You've to wait till the whistle blows
And you can't go in till you hear it
Not even if it snows
And your wellies get filled with water and your socks
    go all soggy and start slipping down your legs

and your hands get so cold they go all
        crumpled and you can't undo
            the buttons of your mac when
                you do get inside . . .
                    . . . it's true.

The best thing is our classroom.
When its fine you can see right far,
Past the Catholic Cathedral
Right to the Morris Car
Works where me Dad works as a fitter and sets off
    right early every morning in these overalls
        with his snap in this sandwich box and
            a flask of tea and always moanin'
                about the money . . . honest.

In Hall we pray for brotherly love
And sing hymns that are ever so long
And the Head shouts at Linda Nutter
Who's always doing wrong.
She can't keep out of trouble because
    she's always talkin'
        she can't stop our teacher says she
            must have been injected with
                a gramaphone needle she talks
                    so much and
    that made me laugh once
            once
        not any more though I've heard it
            too often . . . teachers!

Loving your enemy sounds all right
Until you open your eyes
And you're standing next to Nolan
Who's always telling lies
About me and getting me into trouble and about
   three times a week I fight him after school
      It's like a habit I've got
         but I can't love him even though
           I screw my eyes up real hard and try like
             mad, but if it wasn't him it
              would be somebody else
               I mean
            you've got to have enemies . . .
              . . . haven't you?

We sing 'O to be a pilgrim'
And think about God and heaven
And then we're told the football team lost
By thirteen goals to seven
But that's not bad because St Xavier's don't half have
   big lads in their team and last time we played
      they beat us eighteen one and this time
         we got seven goals . . .
           . . . didn't we?

Then we have our lessons,
We have Science and English and Maths,
Except on Wednesday morning
When our class goes to the baths
And it's not half cold and Peter Bradberry's
   fingers went all wrinkled and blue last week
      and I said, 'You're goin' to die, man'

but he pushed me under the water and I had to
hold my breath for fifteen minutes.
But he's still alive though . . .
. . . he is.

Friday's my favourite day though,
We have Art all afternoon
And I never care what happens
Cos I know it's home-time soon
And I'm free for two whole days but I think
   sometimes it wouldn't be half so good
      having this weekend if we didn't have five
         days
            of
               school
                  in
                     between ___

Would it?

GARETH OWEN

Tom has arranged to meet Huckleberry Finn for an expedition into the graveyard late at night.

At half past nine that night, Tom and Sid were sent to bed as usual. They said their prayers, and Sid was soon asleep. Tom lay awake and waited in restless impatience. When it seemed to him that it must be nearly daylight, he heard the clock strike ten! This was despair. He would have tossed and fidgeted, as his nerves demanded, but he was afraid he might wake Sid. So he lay still and stared up into the dark. Everything was dismally still. By-and-by, out of the stillness little scarcely perceptible noises began to emphasize themselves. The ticking of the clock began to bring itself into notice. Old beams began to crack mysteriously. The stairs creaked faintly. Evidently spirits were abroad. A measured, muffled snore issued from Aunt Polly's chamber. And now the tiresome chirping of a cricket that no human ingenuity could locate began. Next the ghastly ticking of a death-watch in the wall at the bed's head made Tom shudder—it meant that somebody's days were numbered. Then the howl of a far-off dog rose on the night air and was answered by a fainter howl from a remoter distance. Tom was in an agony. At last he was satisfied that time had ceased and eternity begun; he began to doze in spite of himself; the clock chimed eleven, but he did not hear it. And then there came, mingling with his half-formed dreams, a most melancholy caterwauling. The raising of a neighbouring window disturbed him. A cry of 'Scat! you devil!' and the crash of an empty bottle against the back of his aunt's wood-shed brought him wide awake, and a single minute later he was dressed and out of the window and creeping along the roof of the 'ell' on all fours. He 'meow'd' with caution once or twice as he went;

then jumped to the roof of the wood-shed, and thence to the ground. Huckleberry Finn was there, with his dead cat. The boys moved off and disappeared in the gloom. At the end of half an hour they were wading through the tall grass of the graveyard.

It was a graveyard of the old-fashioned western kind. It was on a hill, about a mile and a half from the village. It had a crazy board fence round it, which leaned inward in places, and outward the rest of the time, but stood upright nowhere. Grass and weeds grew rank over the whole cemetery. All the old graves were sunken in. There was not a tombstone on the place; round-topped, worm-eaten boards staggered over the graves, leaning for support and finding none. 'Sacred to the memory of' so-and-so had been painted on them once, but it could no longer have been read, on the most of them, now, even if there had been light.

A faint wind moaned through the trees, and Tom feared it might be the spirits of the dead complaining at being disturbed. The boys talked little, and only under their breath, for the time and the place and the pervading solemnity and silence oppressed their spirits. They found the sharp new heap they were seeking, and ensconced themselves within the protection of three great elms that grew in a bunch within a few feet of the grave.

Then they waited in silence for what seemed a long time. The hooting of a distant owl was all the sound that troubled the dead stillness.

from *Tom Sawyer* by MARK TWAIN

The canal at Coseley

Curling along like a slippery snake,
Runs the canal with its burly bridges,
And lumbering locks grey and creaking,
A home of jumping frogs, nervous newts,
Old iron bedsteads and rusty tin cans,
A watery grave for some unwanted dogs,
The abode of stately swans,
And splashing cygnets,
And rainbow-coloured dragonflies,
Who dive and wheel
Over tall, slender bullrushes,
It is a watery road,
Used by chugging boats,
Carrying loads of coal,
Drums of tar and leaden pipes,
To the Midlands,
From the North,
Steered by unsmiling, lonely men,
Who guide them,
Staring in gloomy silence at us,
As they pass,
It seems as though it will pass away.
For the reeds grow tall,
It needs repairs,
And it soon dies,
But no one cares.

CAROL ELAINE HAWKINS, aged 13

People

Big Goldie

Almost every Saturday night a man comes round to our house they all call Big Goldie. I think they call him that because of his gold teeth he has at the side of his mouth. I noticed this for a long time before I thought that's why they gave him that name. He is certainly a friendly man. 'Hallo, everybody,' he says. 'I got you some presents here somewhere.' And then he looks in his pockets and he can't find anything. He looks in his socks and he can't find anything. 'Well,' he says, 'that is a very funny thing. I know I had them presents when I came out. Now, what could happen to them.' Then he tells a story about how he came along the way and called in at a pub and met a magician who put a spell on him so he wouldn't remember anything. He sits down in the chair and says to my dad, 'Man, them presents is magicked away.' And he does that for some time, shaking his head from side to side but still with his hat on. 'Why don't you take your hat off, Goldie?' My dad says. 'Sitting there in that chair with your hat on like that!' So he looks up quickly and his eyes begin to shine and he takes off his smart black hat and runs his fingers round the edge. 'Well, well, well,' he says. 'What do you think?' And then he takes out some little presents like packets of sweets, or little plastic dolls or something like that. 'I knew there was a spell on me,' he says, then he laughs and balances his hat on the end of his nose. He has everybody in stitches and we always wait for big Goldie on a Saturday night.

SARAH PETRIE, aged 11

David

He is nine years old and lives at Normanton. He is a rough kind of boy with his pullover ruffled up, his shirt hanging half in and half out. He has a tangled mass of hair in knots very untidy. He speaks in a rough mumbling voice with a bit of Yorkshire in it. He has a pair of uncleaned shabby shoes with laces half undone. But on Sundays when he goes to Church he is polite and generous and will share things with you, and he goes with a nice pair of shining shoes and clean hands and face and with a quiff in his hair with a neat parting. When he walks he walks slowly and then he will walk a bit faster. He sniffs a lot because he can't find his handkerchief.

Boy, aged 10

My chimney sweep

Before we went over to electric heating we used to have our chimney swept continually, and what a performance it was. I well remember mother getting up at 7 o'clock in the morning of the sweep's visit, down would come the curtains, ornaments were tucked away, covers went over the chairs, carpet was rolled up and we were ready for his call. Needless to say we were frozen waiting for him to come. Breakfast was snatched out in the little kitchenette, a tiny little room not meant to eat in at all.

Rat a tat, the sweep had arrived. Mother and I go to let him in. He is a funny little man all black, with lots of brushes under his arm. Mother is terrified he will blacken all the paint along the hall, which needless to say he does. Down on the floor he goes chattering all the time about nothing, which enrages my mother when all she wants him to do is clean the chimney and go. He puts rod over rod on the end of the brush, and at last asks us to go in the garden to see if the brush has come through the chimney, this is the moment I love. Also I like it when he takes the brushes down again and there is a lovely pile of dirty black soot in the hearth; how I would love to play with it but no such luck. He shovels it all in a sack, which he throws over his shoulder. Mother's face is black with the soot that is flying about. I am sneezing my head off as soot is up my nose, the only one who is happy is Snow.

As mother pays him he says 'Good morning Madam, I don't think I made too much mess.' Mother grits her teeth and says nothing, but what she says when she closes the door behind the poor little man is nobody's business. All I know is I am glad to go to school out of the way. One day Mummy was in bed ill when we had to have the sweep, so Daddy had to see to the room before and after his visit. I'm sure Mummy was smiling to herself when she heard Dad grumbling away—soon after we had electric fires fitted but they are not much fun really you know.

STEVEN MAXWELL SUTTON, aged 11

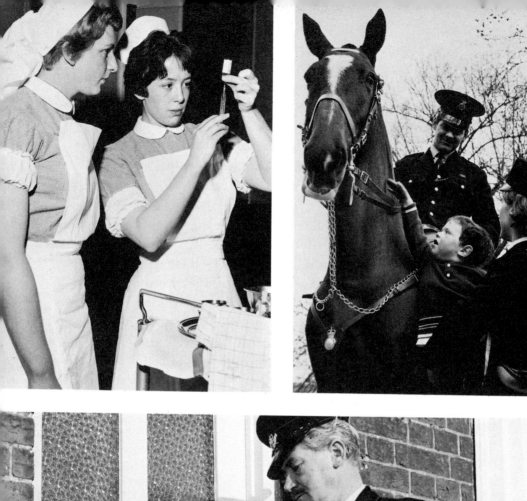

Morning glory

My father would begin each day
By standing in the backyard door
And giving one tremendous sneeze,
Mid-way between a gasp and roar:

Would clap a fist before his eyes,
And give a kind of stamping dance,
As if his spirit wept and sang
To hear such goodly resonance.

And even now I can remember
His gaiters, and the scads of mire
He kicked before him, as this greeting
Sprang from his nostrils like a fire.

And cocks in every neighbouring yard
Would lift their heads, and strut and stir,
Sensing the challenge of some odd,
Irate and twanging chanticlere.

MICHELL RAPER

My papa's waltz

The whiskey on your breath
Could make a small boy dizzy;
But I clung on like death:
Such waltzing was not easy.

We romped until the pans
Slid from the kitchen shelf;
My mother's countenance
Could not unfrown itself.

The hand that held my wrist
Was battered on one knuckle;
At every step you missed
My right ear scraped a buckle.

You beat time on my head
With a palm caked hard by dirt,
Then waltzed me off to bed
Still clinging to your shirt.

THEODORE ROETHKE

An old woman of the roads

Oh, to have a little house!
To own the hearth and stool and all!
The heaped-up sods upon the fire,
The pile of turf against the wall!

To have a clock with weights and chains
And pendulum swinging up and down!
A dresser filled with shining delph,
Speckled and white and blue and brown!

I could be busy all the day
Clearing and sweeping hearth and floor,
And fixing on their shelf again
My white and blue and speckled store!

I could be quiet there at night
Beside the fire and by myself
Sure of a bed and loth to leave
The ticking clock and shining delph!

Och! but I'm weary of mist and dark,
And roads where there's never a house or bush,
And tired I am of bog and road,
And the crying wind and the lonesome hush!

And I am praying to God on high,
And I am praying Him night and day,
For a little house—a house of my own—
Out of the wind's and the rain's way.

PADRAIC COLUM

Just old men

They're slowly plodding up the hill,
Horse and man.
Who can think thoughts, or dream dreams
As they can?
They have time enough to spare,
Horse and man.

A sort of sympathy is shared
Between them;
Much wisdom in each old gray head.
Now and then
The horse's ears twitch happily—
Just old men.

JEAN, aged 11

Denis Law

I live at 14 Stanhope Street,
Me Mum, me Dad and me.
And three of us have made a gang,
John Stokes and Trev and me.

Our favourite day is Saturday;
We go Old Trafford way
And wear red colours in our coats
To watch United play.

We always stand behind the goal
In the middle of the roar.
The others come to see the game—
I come for Denis Law.

His red sleeves flap around his wrists,
He's built all thin and raw,
But the toughest backs don't stand a chance
When the ball's near Denis Law.

He's a whiplash when he's in control,
He can swivel like an eel,
And twist and sprint in such a way
It makes defences reel.

And when he's hurtling for the goal
I know he's got to score.
Defences may stop normal men—
They can't stop Denis Law.

We all race home when full time blows
To kick a tennis ball,
And Trafford Park is our back-yard,
And the stand is next door's wall.

Old Stokesey shouts, 'I'm Jimmy Greaves,'
And scores against the door,
And Trev shouts: 'I'll be Charlton,'—
But I am Denis Law.

GARETH OWEN

Spit Nolan

Spit Nolan was a pal of mine. He was a thin lad with a bony face that was always pale, except for two rosy spots on his cheekbones. He had quick brown eyes, short, wiry hair, rather stooped shoulders, and we all knew that he had only one lung. He had had a disease which in those days couldn't be cured, unless you went away to Switzerland, which Spit certainly couldn't afford. He wasn't sorry for himself in any way, and in fact we envied him, because he never had to go to school.

Spit was the champion trolley-rider of Cotton Pocket; that was the district in which we lived. He had a very good balance, and sharp wits, and he was very brave, so that these qualities, when added to his skill as a rider, meant that no other boy could ever beat Spit on a trolley—and every lad had one.

from *Spit Nolan* by BILL NAUGHTON

The tramp

He limped on like an old ship   *simile*
Entering the breaker's yards,
He staggers along gaunt and ragged
Looking like a fox   *simile*
As he pulls his body across the horizon,
A bent bushy tree.   *metaphore*

93   No man knows where he goes
     To the unknown lands across sheer cliffs
     Which bar all men from their dreams.
     He will be broken to pieces,
     And crumble
     In his grave.

                    JOHN STUART MITCHELL, aged 10

The lonely farmer

Poor hill farmer astray in the grass:
There came a movement and he looked up, but
All that he saw was the wind pass.
There was a sound of voices in the air,
But where, where? It was only the glib stream talking
Softly to itself. And once when he was walking
Along a lane in spring he was deceived
By a shrill whistle coming through the leaves:
Wait a minute, wait a minute—four swift notes;
He turned, and it was nothing, only a thrush
In the thorn bushes easing its throat.
He swore at himself for paying heed,
The poor hill farmer, so often again
Stopping, staring, listening, in vain,
His ear betrayed by the heart's need.

                              R. S. THOMAS

A visit to grandpa's

In the middle of the night I woke up from a dream full of whips and lariats as long as serpents, and runaway coaches on mountain passes, and wide, windy gallops over cactus fields, and I heard the man in the next room crying, 'Gee-up!' and 'Whoa!' and trotting his tongue on the roof of his mouth.

It was the first time I had stayed in grandpa's house. The floor-boards had squeaked like mice as I climbed into bed, and the mice between the walls had creaked like wood as though another visitor was walking on them. It was a mild summer night, but curtains had flapped and branches beaten against the window. I had pulled the sheets over my head, and soon was roaring and riding in a book.

'Whoa there, my beauties!' cried grandpa. His voice sounded very young and loud, and his tongue had powerful hooves, and he made his bedroom into a great meadow. I thought I would see if he was ill, or had set his bedclothes on fire, for my mother had said that he lit his pipe under the blankets, and had warned me to run to his help if I smelt smoke in the night. I went on tiptoe through the darkness to his bedroom door, brushing against the furniture and upsetting a candlestick with a thump. When I saw there was a light in the room I felt frightened, and as I opened the door I heard grandpa shout, 'Gee-up!' as loudly as a bull with a mega-phone.

He was sitting straight up in bed and rocking from side to side as though the bed were on a rough road; the knotted edges of the counterpane were his reins; his invisible horse stood in a shadow beyond the bedside candle. Over a white flannel nightshirt he was wearing a red waistcoat with walnut-sized brass buttons. The over-filled bowl of his pipe smouldered among his whiskers like a little, burning hayrick on a stick. At the sight of me, his hands dropped from the reins and lay blue and quiet, the bed stopped still on a level road, he muffled his tongue into silence, and the horses drew softly up.

'Is there anything the matter, grandpa?' I asked, though the clothes were not on fire. His face in the candlelight looked like a ragged quilt pinned upright on the black air and patched all over with goat-beards.

He stared at me mildly. Then he blew down his pipe, scattering the sparks and making a high, wet dog-whistle of the stem, and shouted: 'Ask no questions.'

After a pause, he said slyly: 'Do you ever have nightmares, boy?'

I said: 'No.'

'Oh, yes, you do,' he said.

I said I was woken by a voice that was shouting to horses.

'What did I tell you?' he said. 'You eat too much. Who ever heard of horses in a bedroom?'

He fumbled under his pillow, brought out a small tinkling bag, and carefully untied its strings. He put a sovereign in my hand, and said: 'Buy a cake.' I thanked him and wished him good night.

As I closed my bedroom door, I heard his voice crying loudly and gaily, 'Gee-up! gee-up!' and the rocking of the travelling bed.

from *Portrait of the Artist as a Young Dog* by DYLAN THOMAS

Georgie and Grandpa

Two of the most interesting characters I have met are my little brother Georgie, aged two months and my great Grandfather aged ninety-seven years two months.

I am interested in both. To my amazement their needs are similar and yet I would have thought that Grandpa would have had fewer needs than Georgie. After all Georgie has need to develop the habits of taking care of himself whereas Grandpa has already learned these things, yet I have heard Mummy say that Georgie is too young to eat meat and Grandpa is now too old for it.

Georgie must be treated with care and gentleness because his bones are weak through lack of age—Grandpa's bones are weak because of over age.

The house must be quiet when Georgie sleeps because he wakens so easily. Grandpa always goes early to bed and otherwise spends much of his time dozing in his rocking-chair.

Grandpa has outgrown the use of a comb and Georgie has not yet grown old enough to need one.

Georgie has not yet the need to a toothbrush. Grandpa stopped cleaning his last remaining tooth four years ago and cannot manage with the new fangled false ones.

Georgie is quite inactive having not yet the strength or ability to walk by himself. Similarly, Grandpa is unable to walk because he has 'screws'!

Little Georgie is without understanding and wisdom, and my Grandfather is past the age of having to understand—his attitude to be wise (as he was a few years ago) is now gone with his memory.

Sounds mean nothing to either of them. Grandfather cannot hear them and Georgie is not yet interested in where they come from or what they mean.

Sometimes Grandpa utters little mumbling noises to himself which mean nothing to either himself or anybody else—unless little Georgie understands them because he also does the same thing—perhaps they are talking to each other in a language of their own!

Both need warmth and are well wrapped up in shawls. Grandpa sucks his pipe while little Georgie sucks his thumb.

Perhaps this is what the adults mean when they say, 'He is a chip off the old block!'—Oh, I forgot to tell you that Grandpa's name is George!

LYNN BOTTOMLEY, aged 10

Huckleberry Finn

Huckleberry was cordially hated and dreaded by all the mothers of the town because he was idle, and lawless, and vulgar, and bad—and because all their children admired him so, and delighted in his forbidden society, and wished they dared to be like him. Tom was like the rest of the respectable boys in that he envied Huckleberry his gaudy outcast condition, and was under strict orders not to play with him. So he played with him every time he got a chance. Huckleberry was always dressed in the cast-off clothes of full-grown men, and they were in perennial bloom and fluttering with rags. His hat was a vast ruin with a wide crescent lopped out of its brim; his coat, when he wore one, hung nearly to his heels, and had the rearward buttons far down the back; but one suspender supported his trousers; the seat of the trousers bagged low and contained nothing; the fringed legs dragged in the dirt when not rolled up. Huckleberry came and went at his own free will. He slept on doorsteps in fine weather, and in empty hogsheads in wet; he did not have to go to school or church, or call any being master, or obey anybody; he could go fishing or swimming when and where he chose, and stay as long as it suited him; nobody forbad him to fight; he could sit up as late as he pleased; he was always the first boy that went barefoot in the spring and the last to resume leather in the fall; he never had to wash, nor put on clean clothes; he could swear wonderfully. In a word, everything that goes to make life precious, that boy had. So thought every hampered, harassed respectable boy in St. Petersburg.

from *Tom Sawyer* by MARK TWAIN

Hernan

Hernan was a very big man with finely developed limbs and a square muscular head. His face was tanned brown by the elements and great strong fair hairs covered the backs of his hands. He was all fairhaired and his face had the gentle, passive expression of the man who never thinks of anything but physical things. An ever-active, fearless man, he was so used to the danger of climbing cliffs that he was as surefooted as a goat. He carried a sack, a heavy short stick and a small basket. The sack was to carry the birds. The stick was used to club them. He stored the eggs in the basket.

from *Trapped* by LIAM O'FLAHERTY

*Lovejoy Mason is a lonely little girl who has made a garden on a sheltered
corner of a bomb-site.*

Tip's camp was the best hidden for miles; screened by a bit of an
old wall, it was like an igloo built of rubble; there was only a
little hole, close to the ground, by which to go in and out; even
the smallest of the boys had to lie down and wriggle. Outside it
looked just another pile of bricks and stones; inside it had bunks
made of orange boxes, an old meat-safe for keeping things in and
an older cooking-stove in which it was possible to light a fire or
heat up a sausage or soup over a candle; drinks were kept in a
hot-water bottle. . . .

The gang had thought the camp completely secret but 'She's
there now,' said Sparkey breathlessly. 'I just seen her go in.'

For a moment they stood still, then Tip put his two little fingers
in the corners of his mouth and whistled. The next moment they
were through the gap, down the bank and in the bomb-ruin.
There was a violent noise of boots on stones, of hoots and cries as
they hunted among the walls, then they found, and Lovejoy was
surrounded.

One minute the garden was there, its stones arranged, the
cornflowers growing, the grass green, the next there were only
boots. To Lovejoy they were boots, though most of the boys wore
shoes, but boys' shoes with heavy steel tips to the soles and heels.
She crouched where she was, while the boys smashed up the
garden, trampled down the grass and kicked away the stones; the
cornflower earth was scattered, the seedlings torn out and pulled
in bits. In a minute no garden was left, and Tip picked up the

trowel and fork and threw them far away across the rubble. 'Now get out,' said Tip to Lovejoy.

Lovejoy stood up; she felt as if she were made of stone, she was so cold and hard, then, in a boy's hand she saw an infinitesimal bit of green; he was rolling a cornflower between his finger and thumb; suddenly her chin began to tremble.

*   *   *

Tip had seen two things the other boys had not; being in front as they attacked, he had seen the garden whole; he had not had time to look properly but he had a vision of something laid out, green and alive, carefully edged with stones; the other thing he had seen, and saw now, only he did not want to look was the trembling of Lovejoy's chin. She had not uttered a sound, not screamed, or cried or protested; the Malones were vociferous, Tip connected females with screams and cries and here was only this small trembling. It made him feel uncomfortable; he remembered how a puppy's legs, when he had seen it run over and killed, had trembled like that.

'Get out,' he said to Lovejoy but less fiercely. As she still seemed dazed he put his hand on her shoulder to turn her but he should have known better than to touch her . . . she turned her head and bit Tip's hand.

She bit as hard as she could, and ran.

*   *   *

It was an hour or two later that Cassie burst into the Masons' room. She never knocked. One does not knock for children.

'There's a boy wants to see you,' she told Lovejoy.

'I don't want to see a boy,' said Lovejoy.

'Hoity-toity!' said Cassie. 'Well, I'm making a cup of tea … You'd better come down and have yours now.'

'I don't want any tea.'

'Don't you feel well?' asked curious Cassie.

'Quite well,' said Lovejoy but she felt neither well nor ill; she felt nothing, nothing at all; she might have been dead. 'You can come down or go to bed,' said Cassie.

Lovejoy came down ... Her fingers gripped in her pocket, found the pill-box. Thoughtfully she took it outside and emptied it down the gutter.

The seeds fell down like rain; she wondered if they would stick in the gutter and grow, and she thought of nasturtiums flowering on the pavement edges and at once the familiar feeling stirred in her, the garden feeling. But what's the use of that now? Lovejoy was thinking wearily, when a boy came up from the shadow by the side door. It was Tip.

Lovejoy stiffened. 'What do you want?' she said, backing against the house wall.

Tip did not see why she should flinch and back away like that. He had not hurt her, while she had left a half-circle of bleeding little purple marks on his hand. 'The first thing she ever did for me she bit me,' he was to say afterwards. The bite ached still. Nor did he at all understand why he was doing what he did now. 'I came back to bring you this,' he said and held out the garden fork. 'I couldn't find the trowel,' said Tip, 'but we've got a little old shovel you could use.'

Lovejoy made no attempt to hold the fork; as she walked away to the edge of the pavement she let it drop from her hand into the gutter; then she sat down on the kerb and began to cry.

Tip was one of those boys who are so big and strong that people do not really look at them; they look at their boots, their big young knees and shoulders, their jaws perhaps, but not at them. 'What a young tough!' people said of Tip, but Mrs Malone, who knew him better than anyone else, said, 'He's not tough. He's gentle.' Few people divined this. Yet Lovejoy divined it, at once.

To Lovejoy Tip was a bitter-enemy boy, the biggest and worst of the ones who had smashed her garden, and yet she, who never cried in front of anyone, who had not cried then, was moved to cry now, in front of him. He did not jeer at her, nor did he go away embarrassed; he picked up the fork and sat down on the kerb beside her.

from An Episode of Sparrows by Rumer Godden

A was an Archer
    who shot at a frog

B was a Butcher
    who kept a bull-dog

C was a Captain
    all covered with lace

D was a Drummer
    who played with much grace

E   was an Esquire
with pride on his brow

F   was a Farmer
who followed the plough

G   was a Gamster
who had but ill-luck

H   was a Hunter
and hunted a buck

I   was an Italian
who had a white mouse

J   was a Joiner
and built up a house

K   was a King
so mighty and grand

L   was a Lady
who had a white hand

M   was a Miser
who hoarded up gold

N   was a Nobleman
gallant and bold

O   was an Organ boy
who played about town

P was a Parson
who wore a black gown

Q was a Queen
who was fond of her people

R was a Robin
who perched on a steeple

S was a Sailor
who spent all he got

T was a Tinker
who mended a pot

U was an Usher
who taught little boys

V was a Vetran
who sold pretty toys

W was a Watchman
who guarded the door

X was eXpensive
and so became poor

Y was a Youth
who did not love school

Z was a Zany
who looked a great fool.

Anon.

Jargon

Jerusalem, Joppa, Jericho—
These are the cities of long ago.

Jasper, jacinth, jet and jade—
Of such are jewels for ladies made.

Juniper's green and jasmine's white,
Sweet jonquil is spring's delight.

Joseph, Jeremy, Jennifer, James,
Julian, Juliet—just names.

January, July and June—
Birthday late or birthday soon.

Jacket, jersey, jerkin, jeans—
What's the wear for sweet sixteens?

Jaguar, jackel, jumbo, jay—
Came to dinner but couldn't stay.

Jellies, junkets, jumbals, jam—
Mix them up for sweet-toothed Sam.

To jig, to jaunt, to jostle, to jest—
These are the things that Jack loves best.

Jazz, jamboree, jubilee, joke—
The jolliest words you ever spoke.

From A to Z and Z to A
The joyfullest letter of all is J.

JAMES REEVES

The man in the wilderness

The man in the wilderness asked of me,
How many strawberries grow in the sea?
I answered him as I thought good,
As many red herrings as grow in the wood.

Anon.

If elephants were as small as insects
If ants were as big as whales
If sharks could fly
Like mice in the sky
Then horses would run like snails.

MARTIN, aged 10

I dreamed a dream next Tuesday week,
Beneath the apple-trees;
I thought my eyes were big pork-pies,
And my nose was Stilton cheese.
The clock struck twenty minutes to six,
When a frog sat on my knee;
I asked him to lend me eighteenpence,
But he borrowed a shilling of me.

Anon.

Infir taris
Inoak nonis,
Inmudeelsis,
In claynonis.
Cana goateati vi?
Cana maretots?

Anon.

Civile, res ago
Fortibus es in ero.
Gnoses mare, Thebe trux.
Vatis inem?
Causan dux.

Anon.

There was a man, he went mad,
He jumped into a paper bag;
The paper bag was too narrow,
He jumped into a wheelbarrow;
The wheelbarrow took on fire,
He jumped into a cow byre;
The cow byre was too nasty,
He jumped into an apple pasty;
The apple pasty was too sweet,
He jumped into Chester-le-Street;
Chester-le-Street was full of stones,
He fell down and broke his bones.

Anon.

The end of the road

In these boots and with this staff
Two hundred leaguers and a half
Walked I, went I, paced I, tripped I,
Marched I, held I, skelped I, slipped I,
Pushed I, panted, swung and dashed I;
Picked I, forded, swam and splashed I,
Strolled I, climbed I, crawled and scrambled,
Dropped and dipped I, ranged and rambled;
Plodded I, hobbled I, trudged and tramped I,
And in lonely spinnies camped I,
Lingered, loitered, limped and crept I,
Clambered, halted, stepped and leapt I,
Slowly sauntered, roundly strode I,
    And . . .
    Let me not conceal it . . . rode I.

from The End of the Road by HILAIRE BELLOC

Waterfall

Dividing and gliding and sliding,
And falling and brawling and sprawling,
And diving and riving and striving,
And sprinkling and twinkling and wrinkling,
And sounding and bounding and rounding,
And bubbling and troubling and doubling,
And grumbling and rumbling and tumbling,
And clattering and battering and shattering;
Retreating and beating and meeting and sheeting,
Delaying and straying and playing and spraying,
Advancing and prancing and glancing and dancing . . .

from *The Cataract at Lodore* by ROBERT SOUTHEY

Jump or jiggle

Frogs jump
Caterpillars hump

Worms wiggle
Bugs jiggle

Rabbits hop
Horses clop

Snakes slide
Sea-gulls glide

Mice creep
Deer leap

Puppies bounce
Kittens pounce

Lions stalk—
But—
I *walk*!

EVELYN BEYER

Cuckoo

Cuckoo, Cuckoo,
What do you do?

In April
I open my bill

In May
I sing night and day.

In June
I change my tune.

In July
Up high I fly.

In August
Away I must.

Anon.

Severe frost

waterfowl
water

waterfowl
ice
water

waterfowl
ice
ice

icefowl
ice
ice

ice
ice
ice

ice
ice
ice

ice

Through winter

GOLDFINCH
COLDFINCH
SNOWFINCH
HOARFINCH
THAWFINCH

NIPPERY
DIPPERY
FISHERY
WHISKERY
DRIPPERY
FLICKERY
SEALIPPERY

Snowblind

Articfox
Was it,
Making trax
In the snow?
Or did my ice
Play trix?

GEOFFREY SUMMERFIELD

What woke the boy up.

~~What~~ How many times had he stayed at Grandpa's house.

What sound had the floorboards made when he had walked on them.

What time of year was it.

What was the weather like that night

Why did the boy think that Grandpa's bedclothes might be on fire

What did the boy knock over on his way to Grandpa's room

What was Grandpa using as reins

What was Grandpa wearing.

How is his pipe described

What does Grandpa first reply to the boy's enquiry

What excuse does Grandpa give to make the boy think he was just imagining things

What did Grandpa give the boy.

Cabbage-bite

FIND LEAF
EAT LEAF
LEAF MEAL
PIECEMEAL
LEAVELEAF
ALL HOLE

Dayflight

Thrushrush
Beakpoke
Stonestun
Snapsnail
Draindrop
Shellshed

GEOFFREY SUMMERFIELD

One old ox

One old ox opening oysters,
Two toads totally tired
Trying to trot to Tewkesbury,
Three tame tigers taking tea,
Four fat friars fishing for frogs,
Five fairies finding fire-flies,
Six soldiers shooting snipe,
Seven salmon sailing in Solway,
Eight elegant engineers eating excellent eggs;
Nine nimble noblemen nibbling non-pareils,
Ten tall tinkers tasting tamarinds,
Eleven electors eating early endive,
Twelve tremendous tale-bearers telling truth.

ANON.

There was an old woman

There was an old woman who swallowed a fly:
I wonder why
She swallowed a fly.
Poor old woman, she's sure to die.
There was an old woman who swallowed a spider,
That wriggled and wiggled right down inside her;
She swallowed the spider to catch the fly,
But I don't know why
She swallowed the fly.
Poor old woman, she's sure to die.

There was an old woman who swallowed a bird;
How absurd to swallow a bird!
She swallowed the bird to catch the spider,
That wriggled and wiggled right down inside her;
She swallowed the spider to catch the fly,
But I don't know why
She swallowed the fly.
Perhaps she'll die.

There was an old woman who swallowed a cat;
Fancy that!
She swallowed a cat!
She swallowed the cat to catch the bird,
She swallowed the bird to catch the spider,
That wriggled and wiggled right down inside her;
She swallowed the spider to catch the fly;
Now I wonder why
She swallowed that fly.
Maybe she'll die.

117 There was an old woman who swallowed a dog;
She went the whole hog
And swallowed a dog.
She swallowed the dog to catch the cat,
She swallowed the cat to catch the bird,
She swallowed the bird to catch the spider,
That wriggled and wiggled deep down inside her;
She swallowed the spider to catch the fly,
But I don't know why
She swallowed a fly.
Could be she'll die.

There was an old woman who swallowed a cow;
Now I don't know how
She swallowed a cow.
She swallowed the cow to catch the dog,
She swallowed the dog to catch the cat,
She swallowed the cat to catch the bird,
She swallowed the bird to catch the spider
That wriggled and wiggled deep down inside her;
She swallowed the spider to catch the fly,
I couldn't say why
She swallowed the fly.
She's sure to die.

There was an old woman who swallowed a horse;
She's dead, of course!

Anon.

The eveni ctual g em

r
a a
t
s p
u
g n c
n
shines
s h
i n
e s
m
e
d
a
l
i r a j i
k a a h' d
e s

I hear the whistle of
the   the bird
beautiful bird of prey

I see far away
the cathedral

GUILLAUME APOLLINAIRE

I
a m
round and the
go they wind r o
t h e u h
d a l e r t i l l m e u n e
I n m y t i g h t I p d.
a s r e v t e g s c
g. y e k d n a r e l l a m h T l
n e h t n r u t y o
i r p s s' k c

SIMON, aged 10

A boa-constrictor goes
a
gliding
all quietly
zig-
zag
zig-
zag
through
the rough grass then
he sees
a
young antelope . . .
He opens his great big jaws and swallows it
gallupps
down
goes it
smaller and smaller till there's
nothing left

LESLEY, aged 11

Swatted between bats
The celluloid ball
Leaps on unseen elastic
Skimming the taut net.
Sliced   Spun
Screwed   Cut
Dabbed   Smashed
      Point
        Service
Ping   Pong
  Pong   Ping
Bing   bong
Bong   Bing
      Point
        Service
  Ding   Dong
  Dong   Ding
Ting   Tong
Tang   Tong
      Point
      Service
  Angled   Slipped
Cut   Driven
Floated   Caressed
  Driven   Hammered

  THWACKED
      Point
      Service
Bit   Bat

```
Tip      Tap
   Slip        Slap
Zip      Zap
Whip     Whap
           Point
         Service
   Left      Yes
Right       Yes
Twist       Yes
Skids        Yes
Eighteen    Seventeen
Eighteen    All
Nineteen        Eighteen
Ninteen         All
Twenty          Nineteen
           Point
         Service
Forehand    Backhand
Swerves     Yes
Rockets     Yes
Battered        Ah
Cracked         Ah
      SMASHED
        SMASHED
          SMASHED
      GAME.
```

GARETH OWEN

A riddle

Silent is my dress when I step across the earth,
Reside in my house, or ruffle the waters.
Sometimes my adornments and this high windy air
Lift me over the livings of men,
The power of the clouds carries me far
Over all people. My white pinions
Resound very loudly, ring with a melody,
Sing out clearly, when I sleep not on
The soil or settle on grey waters . . . a travelling spirit.

Anglo-Saxon riddle
Translated by KEVIN CROSSLEY-HOLLAND

A riddle

This wind wafts little creatures
High over the hill-slopes. They are very
Swarthy, clad in coats of black.
They travel here and there in hordes all together,
Singing loudly, liberal with their songs.
Their haunts are wooded cliffs, yet they sometimes
Come to the houses of men. Name them yourselves.

Anglo-Saxon riddle
Translated by KEVIN CROSSLEY-HOLLAND

f   u   th   o   r   c   g   w   h   n   i   j   e   p

Grey

Grey is the sky, and grey the woodman's cot
With grey smoke tumbling from the chimney-pot.
The flagstones are grey that lead to the door;
Grey is the hearth, and grey the worn old floor.

The old man by the fire nods in his chair;
Grey are his clothes and grey his silvery hair.
Grey are the shadows around him creeping,
And grey the mouse from the corner peeping.

JAMES REEVES

Grey

Grey is the evil heart, in the thundering grey sky.
Grey is the bowed old head that waits its turn to die.
Grey are the rocks that are whipped by the groaning sea.
Grey is the perilous path that leads to the cavern of demons.
Grey is the silken webb of the spider of old.
Grey are the eyes that watch the world go by on T.V.
The mourning star is as grey as the clouds that wander, wander to
the end,

To the end of the world.

CAROL, aged 11

| x | s | t | b | e | ng | d | l | m | œ | ɑ | æ | y | eɑ |

Slowly

Slowly the tide creeps up the sand,
Slowly the shadows cross the land.
Slowly the cart-horse pulls his mile,
Slowly the old man mounts the stile.

Slowly the hands move round the clock,
Slowly the dew dries on the dock.
Slow is the snail—but slowest of all
The green moss spreads on the old brick wall.

JAMES REEVES

The rain dance

The fire flickered with a flare,
The ghostly figure leapt in the air.
Huge shadows fell across the ground
When the figure landed without any sound.
A piercing scream, a bongo beat,
A tossing head, two stamping feet,
Legs bent at knees, feet wide apart,
A twisting body, a thudding heart.
The drums beat out, loud and clear.
D-rr-um-dum-dum, the time draws near.
The twirling body leaps again
Trying hard to make it rain.

MARINA BRUNSKILL, aged 14

Activities

Through the tunnel

Jerry has seen bigger boys diving into the water and coming up the other side of a rock. He realises that they must be swimming through a tunnel and forces himself to try it.

But even after he had made the decision, or thought he had, he found himself sitting up on the rock and looking down into the water, and he knew that now, this moment, when his nose had only just stopped bleeding, when his head was still sore and throbbing—this was the moment when he would try. If he did not do it now, he never would. He was trembling with fear that he would not go, and he was trembling with horror at that long, long tunnel under the rock, under the sea. Even in the open sun-light the barrier rock seemed very wide and very heavy; tons of rock pressed down on where he would go. If he died there he would lie until one day—perhaps not before next year—those big boys would swim into it and find it blocked.

He put on his goggles, fitted them tight, tested the vacuum. His hands were shaking. Then he chose the biggest stone he could carry and slipped over the edge of the rock until half of him was in the cool, enclosing water and half in the hot sun. He looked up once at the empty sky, filled his lungs once, twice, and then sank

fast to the bottom with the stone. He let it go and began to count.
He took the edges of the hole in his hands and drew himself into
it, wriggling his shoulders in sideways as he remembered he
must, kicking himself along with his feet.

Soon he was clear inside. He was in a small rock-bound hole
filled with yellowish-grey water. The water was pushing him up
against the roof. The roof was sharp and pained his back. He pulled
himself along with his hands—fast, fast—and used his legs as
levers. His head knocked against something; a sharp pain dizzied
him. Fifty, fifty-one, fifty-two . . . He was without light, and the
water seemed to press upon him with the weight of the rock.
Seventy-one, seventy-two . . . There was no strain on his lungs.
He felt like an inflated balloon, his lungs were so light and easy,
but his head was pulsing.

He was being continually pressed against the sharp roof, which
felt slimy as well as sharp. Again he thought of octopuses, and
wondered if the tunnel might be filled with weed that could tangle
him. He gave a panicky, convulsive kick forward, ducked his
head, and swam. His feet and hands moved freely, as if in open
water. The hole must have widened out. He thought he must be
swimming fast, and he was frightened of banging his head if the
tunnel narrowed.

A hundred, a hundred and one . . . The water paled. Victory
filled him. His lungs were beginning to hurt. A few more strokes
and he would be out. He was counting wildly; he said a hundred
and fifteen, and then, a long time later, a hundred and fifteen
again. The water was a clear jewel-green all around him. Then
he saw, above his head, a crack running up through the rock.
Sunlight was falling through it, showing the clean dark rock of
the tunnel, a single mussel shell, and darkness ahead.

He was at the end of what he could do. He looked up at the crack
as if it were filled with air and not water, as if he could put his

mouth to it and draw in air. A hundred and fifteen, he heard himself say inside his head—but he had said that long ago. He must go on into the blackness ahead, or he would drown. His head was swelling, his lungs cracking. A hundred and fifteen, a hundred and fifteen pounded through his head, and he feebly clutched at rocks in the dark, pulling himself forward, leaving the brief space of sunlit water behind. He felt he was dying. He was no longer quite conscious. He struggled on in the darkness between lapses into unconsciousness. An immense, swelling pain filled his head, and then the darkness cracked with an explosion of green light. His hands, groping forward, met nothing, and his feet, kicking back, propelled him out into the open sea.

He drifted to the surface, his face turned up to the air. He was gasping like a fish. He felt he would sink now and drown; he could not swim the few feet back to the rock. Then he was clutching it and pulling himself on to it. He lay face down, gasping. He could see nothing but a red-veined, clotted dark. His eyes must have burst, he thought; they were full of blood. He tore off his goggles and a gout of blood went into the sea. His nose was bleeding, and the blood had filled his goggles.

from *The Habit of Loving* by DORIS LESSING

The Summit

Hillary and Tenzing are close to the summit of Everest

Taking advantage of every little rockhold and all the force of knee, shoulder and arms I could muster, I literally cramponed backwards up the crack, with a fervent prayer that the cornice would remain attached to the rock. Despite the considerable effort involved, my progress although slow was steady, and as

Tenzing paid out the rope, I inched my way upwards until I could finally reach over the top of the rock and drag myself out of the crack on to a wide ledge.

For a few moments I lay regaining my breath and for the first time really felt the fierce determination that nothing now could stop us reaching the top. I took a firm stance on the ledge and signalled to Tenzing to come on up. As I heaved hard on the rope Tenzing wriggled his way up the crack and finally collapsed exhausted at the top, like a giant fish when it has just been hauled from the sea after a terrible struggle.

I checked both our oxygen sets and roughly calculated our flow rates. Everything seemed to be going well. Probably owing to the strain imposed on him by the trouble with his oxygen set, Tenzing had been moving rather slowly; but he was climbing safely, and this was the major consideration. His only comment on my en-quiring of his condition was to smile and wave along the ridge.

The ridge continued as before. Giant cornices on the right, steep rock slopes on the left. I went on cutting steps on the narrow strip of snow. The ridge curved away to the right and we had no idea where the top was. As I cut around the back of one hump, another higher one would swing into view. Time was passing and the ridge seemed never-ending.

In one place where the angle of the ridge had eased off, I tried cramponing without cutting steps, hoping this would save time. But I quickly realized that our margin of safety on these steep slopes at this altitude was too small, so I went on step-cutting.

I was beginning to tire a little now. I had been cutting steps continuously for two hours, and Tenzing, too, was moving very slowly. As I chipped steps around still another corner, I wondered rather dully just how long we could keep it up.

Our original zest had now quite gone and it was turning more into a grim struggle. I then realized that the ridge ahead, instead of still monotonously rising, now dropped sharply away, and far below I could see the North Col and the Rongbuk Glacier. I looked upwards to see a narrow snow ridge running up to a snowy summit. *A few more whacks of the ice-axe in the firm snow and we stood on top.*

My initial feelings were of relief—relief that there were no more steps to cut—no more ridges to traverse—no more humps to tantalize us with hopes of success. I looked at Tenzing and in spite of the balaclava, goggles and oxygen mask, all encrusted with long icicles that concealed his face, there was no disguising his infectious grin of pure delight as he looked all around him. We shook hands and then Tenzing threw his arm around my shoulders and we thumped each other on the back until we were almost breathless. It was 11.30 a.m. The ridge had taken us two and a half hours, but it seemed like a lifetime.

from *The Ascent of Everest* by EDMUND HILLARY

Breathless

Written at 21,200 feet on May 23rd 1953 Climbing Everest

Heart aches,
Lungs pant
The dry air
Sorry, scant.
Legs lift
And why at all?
Loose drift,
Heavy fall.
Prod the snow

Its easiest way;
A flat step
Is holiday.
Look up,
The far stone
Is many miles
Far and alone.
Grind the breath
Once more and on;
Don't look up
Till journey's done.
Must look up,
Glasses are dim.
Wrench of hand
Is breathless limb.
Pause one step,
Breath swings back;
Swallow once,
Dry throat is slack.
Then on
To the far stone;
Don't look up,
Counts the steps done.
One step,
One heart-beat,
Stone no nearer
Dragging feet.
Heart aches,
Lungs pant
The dry air
Sorry, scant.

WILFRID NOYCE

The fight

The kick off is
I don't like him;
Nothing about him.
He's fat and soft,
Like a jellybaby he is.
Now he's never done nothing,
Not to me,
He wouldn't dare:
Nothing at all of anything like that.
I just can't stand him,
So I'll fight him
And I'll beat him,
I could beat him any day.

The kick off is it's his knees:
They knock together,
They sock together.
And they're fat,
With veins that run into his socks
Too high.
Like a girl he is,
And his shorts,
Too long,
They look
All wrong,
Like a Mummy's boy.
Then
He simpers and dimples,
Like a big lass he is;
So I'll fight him

Everyone beats him,
I could beat him any day.

For another thing it's his hair,
All smarmed and oily fair,
All silk and parted flat,
His Mum does it like that
With her flat hand and water,
All licked and spittled into place,
With the quiff all down his face.
And his satchel's new
With his name in blue
Chalked on it.
So I chalked on it,
'Trevor is a cissie'
On it.
So he's going to fight me,
But I'll beat him,
I could beat him any day.

There's a crowd behind the sheds
When we come they turn their heads
Shouting and laughing,
Wanting blood and a bashing.
Take off my coat, rush him,
Smash him, bash him
Lash him, crash him
In the head,
In the bread
Basket.
Crack, thwack,
He's hit me back

Shout and scream
'Gerroff me back,
Gerroff, gerroff!
You wait, I'll get you,
I could beat you any day!'

Swing punch, bit his hand.
Blood on teeth, blood on sand.
Buttons tear, shouts and sighs,
Running nose, tears in eyes.
I'll get him yet; smack him yet.
Smash his smile, teacher's pet.
Brow grazed by knuckle
Knees begin to buckle.
'Gerroff me arms your hurtin' me!'
'Give in?'
'No.'
'Give in?'
'No. Gerroff me arms!'
'Give in?'
'No.'
'Give in?'
'GIVE IN?'
'NEVER.'
'GIVE IN?'
'OOOH GERROOFF GERROFF.'
'GIVE IN?'
'I . . . give . . . in . . . yeah.'

Don't cry, don't cry,
Wipe tears from your eye.
Walk home all alone

In the gutters all alone.
Next time I'll send him flying,
I wasn't really trying;
I could beat him any day.

GARETH OWEN

The fight

I had never had a fight before. I felt important and pleased at the crowds who were round us, none of them touching us but leaving it to us to have our fight.

'Back a bit,' I said, and I was right pleased when they moved back. I took off my coat and handed it to a kid I did not know. He took it and held it carefully over his arm, and this pleased me too.

Raymond Garnett took off his coat and his glasses. I had never seen him without his glasses before, except that time when we were playing in Clarkson's woods with Marion. He had a white mark on his nose where he had taken them off and it gave me a feeling that I could bash him easy. He gave them to a kid to look after and as the crowd started pushing the kid went: '*Mi-ind* his glasses!'

We both stepped forward to meet each other and put our fists up. We stood staring at each other and dancing round a bit like they do on the pictures, then I shot out my right hand to Garnett's chin but it missed and caught his shoulder. The next thing I knew was that his fist had caught me a stinging clout over the forehead. I was suprised and worried at the size of the blow and I began to notice, in a far-off sort of way, that he was a lot bigger than me and that his arms were thicker and longer.

I don't know how I got time to look at the people in the ring around us, but I did, and I noticed that I didn't even *know* most of them. Little Rayner was at the front shouting: 'Go it, Garno!' and this hurt me, don't ask my why. Ted was at the back, jumping up and down to get a good look.

I started trying to remember what people had told me about fighting. I knew you had to hit a man on his shoulders so as to weaken his arms, and another trick was to pretend to hit him in

the belly and then when his arms went down, well you get him in
the face instead. They didn't work. I hit Garno twice on his right
shoulder and he didn't feel anything, and when I tried to go for
his belly my own arms were down and he hit me on the lip. I
could feel it swelling already and I heard the crowd go: 'Ohhhhh!'
I suddenly realised that I had made a mistake and that Garno
was tougher than I was and he was going to wipe the blinking
floor with me and there was nothing I could do about it.

I remembered reading in the *Hotspur* or somewhere about all
these boxers, they always hit with their left. I tried to hit Garno
with my left but I couldn't aim it properly and I missed. Little
Rayner started going: 'Cur, call this a fight!' One or two kids
at the back had started their own little fights.

I started trying to look in Garno's eyes all the time. This was
something else I remembered. If you look the other man in the
eyes all the time, well you can tell what he's going to do.

You couldn't tell what blinking *Garno* was going to do. He
seemed surprised that I was staring at him all the time, and for a
minute I thought he was going to start saying: 'Have you seen all?'
His mouth was pursed up and he looked as though he was getting
his mad up. Suddenly, for no reason at all as far as I could see,
he went: 'Right! You've asked for it now!' and he started laying
into me. I started dancing round backwards like proper boxers
do. There was a bump or a stone or something and I tripped over
and fell, sprawling. Little Rayner shouted: 'What you doing on
the floor, man?' Garno stood over me, breathing though his
mouth.

'Do you give in?' he said.

The question seemed cocky and unfair. I said: 'We haven't
started yet!' I got on my feet and he hit me with his fist in the face.
I didn't fall this time but I turned round to stop him hitting me.
I was all hunched up and almost cringing and I could feel his

knuckles on the back of my head. Some kids were drifting away from the back of the crowd and that was even worse. Ted at the back started shouting: 'One-two-three-four, who-are-*we*-for-GARno!' Nobody took up the cry and he sounded silly.

Garno had stopped moving round the ring now. He just stood there and every time I came near him he hit me. He hit me on the lip again and it started bleeding.

We stood staring at each other, our fists clenched, breathing heavily. I said to the kid who had my coat: 'Get us my hanky.' because the blood was going down my chin.

The kid said: 'Clean your boots for fourpence.' He dropped my coat on the floor and started going: 'Yurrrks!' as though it were all over lice or something.

'Do you give in?' said Raymond Garnett.

I didn't answer him, I couldn't. Suddenly Garno lifted his hand and slapped me across the cheek. It wasn't with his fist, it was with his open hand. I had to bite into my bleeding lip to stop myself from crying. The tears came up into my eyes.

'*So-ock* him, man!' said Little Rayner.

'Do you give in?' said Raymond Garnett. He slapped me across the face again. I couldn't stop the tears rolling down my cheeks.

'Yer,' I muttered.

Garnett started dusting his hands together and said: 'Right, that's that, then!' And then from the back Ted shouted: 'He's still got his fists up, Garno!' Hurriedly I let my fists go and dropped my hands to my side. 'Do you want any more?' said Garno. 'No,' I said. 'Right,' he said again. 'That's that, then!'

He took his glasses from the kid who was holding them and put them on, pulling the wire up so that it went over his ears. He did not put his coat on but held it over his arms as he walked away. One or two kids patted him on the back and said: 'Good old you, man!' Nobody said anything to me and I picked my coat up off

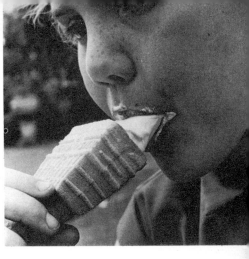

the floor and they began to drift away.

I walked across the field in the direction of Parkside. Once I thought I heard Little Rayner shouting after me: 'Laddy-lass!' but I could not be sure.

from *There is a Happy Land* by KEITH WATERHOUSE

Windy boy in a windswept tree

The branch swayed, swerved,
Swept and whipped, up,
Down, right to left,
Then leapt to right again,
As if to hurl him down
To smash to smithereens
On the knife-edge grass
Or smother
In the close-knit quilts of moss.
Out on a crazy limb
He screwed his eyes tight shut,
To keep out the dizzy ground.
Sweat greased his palms;
Fear pricked his forehead.
The twisted branches lunged and lurched,
His body curved, twisted, he arched
His legs and gripped the bark

143   Between his ankles.
The crust of bark
Sharp as glasspaper
And rough with wrinkles
Grazed his skin
And raised the raw red flesh
And crazed his mind
With fear of breaking.
Then the mad-cap, capering wind
Dropped.
The branch steadied,
Paused,
Rested.
He slowly clambered, slowly back,
Slowly so safely,
Then dropped
Like a wet blanket
To the rick-like, reassuring ground.
Finally, without a sound
He walked carefully
Home.

GEOFFREY SUMMERFIELD

The fly

The fly's sick whining buzz
Appals me as I sit
Alone and quietly,
Reading and hearing it
Banging against the pane,
Bruised, falling, then again
Starting its lariat tour
Round and round my head
Ceiling to wall to floor.

But I equip myself
To send him on his way,
Newspaper clutched in hand
Vigilant, since he may
Settle, shut off his shriek
And there lie mild and weak
Who thirty seconds ago
Drove air and ears mad
With shunting to and fro.

from *The Fly* by ANTHONY THWAITE

Moth

I sometimes lie reading my books in bed
Where it is very quiet,
There I can concentrate in the silence.
Then the idiot moth blunders in.
He thumps against the light fluttering his wings.
Round and round he goes, swinging, and thumping,
Banging and stuttering into the light bulb.
He must be stupid to keep bashing himself at the bulb.
It takes my mind off my books and I cannot concentrate.
All I can think of is the noise of this moth
Fluttering, whirring, swizzing, flickering,
Until I get out of bed and throw something.
That stops him. It is a shame really.

MAURICE, aged 11

The pond

A slimy, green frog on the rippled water,
A small boy playing in the slimy sand,
Edging the round, green pond.
Situated in the centre of the countryside,
A most wonderful scene.
The boy's chubby hand reaches out,
Aiming at the slimy frog.
Then suddenly, plop! and then . . .
Then the frog is gone.
The small boy turns and walks away.
All is peaceful once more.

Boy, aged 11

Peeling an apple

I chose a green apple from the dish and I could tell it was crisp as there was not a blemish on it and it was as immaculate as a city gent. I thought I would see if I could peel it in one go. I carefully selected a sharp knife and began to peel very slowly from the top down. I had to get the knife at an angle to get round the short stubby stalk. Having got past there I carefully went round the apple holding it in my left hand and making a circular motion with both hands. The peel began to come away in some places. It was very thin and almost broke as it dangled down from the top of the apple. The knife began to go deep and I had to pull it towards me but not too much. As I pulled it I became tense and almost desperate not wanting to spoil my efforts. It became dangerously thin and some green tinges of skin were left on the apple. I went on peeling and mummy said that I was motionless as I sat on the floor. As I came to near the end I turned the apple upside-down so as not to be at an angle. The apple was wet and cold in my hand and felt like a stone wrapped in paper tissues and wetted. With only about an inch to go the knife came too close to the surface and the skin split. All my efforts had been in vain. I felt as though I had flopped an exam, I didn't know why, I just did. Maybe it was because I had put a lot into it.

LINDA PIESLEY, aged 12

Waiting

Waiting, waiting, waiting
  For the party to begin;
Waiting, waiting, waiting
  For the laughter and din;

Waiting, waiting, waiting
   With hair just so
And clothes trim and tidy
   From top-knot to toe.
The floor is all shiny,
   The lights are ablaze;
There are sweetmeats in plenty
   And cakes beyond praise.
Oh the games and dancing,
   The tricks and the toys
The music and the madness
   The colour and noise!
Waiting, waiting, waiting
   For the first knock on the door—
Was ever such waiting,
   Such waiting before?

JAMES REEVES

Time

The car stands still
As if it had never been driven.
People walk with their prams,
A dog runs down with a grin on his face.
The cross on the church reminds you of happy days
While seagulls stick their tummies out like heroes.

REG COWIE, aged 8

Going to the shop

One day I got sent to the shop to buy some things. I had to get some sugar, some butter and some flour. I had it written down on a piece of card. My mother gave me a ten-shilling note and I held it tightly in my hand. It was such a fine day when I went out to the shop. There were some children playing hopscotch in the street. They called me. They said, 'Come on and play, Billy.' So I went over the road to have a look. They were all having a good play and I joined in for a bit. Then I went and stopped to watch some kids playing marbles. They had some new ones with brown and green stripes in them and they let me play with them for a bit so we had a talk about it and I said I'd swap two big ones for a green one. Then we played leap frog for a bit. All of a sudden I remembered what I'd gone out for and I'd been playing for ages and I expected mom to come looking for me any minute. Then I should be for it if she found out I'd been playing all the time. I had to run off to the shop fast. When I got to the shop it was full of customers all talking and they keep you waiting. I thought I'd never get served with all the women talking. It gets on your nerves when they all keep you waiting. I could have got served myself if they would let me. Well in the end I got served and I put the things in the bag and I looked for my money in my hand, AND IT WAS NOT THERE. I felt in my pockets AND IT WAS NOT THERE. I started to cry a bit because I had lost it. I must have lost it when I was playing in the street. The shop-keeper said, 'What's the matter, sonny?' and I told him I'd lost the money in the street and he said, 'Well, you'd better go and find it.' I ran all the way to where I was playing and I was crying a lot. I saw one of the big boys had got my ten shillings and I said, 'That's mine. I left it playing.' And he wouldn't give it me so I said, 'If you don't give it me I'll tell my uncle Sam, he's a policeman.' And the girl said, 'Give it him back, Roger.' After a bit he let me have it and I was so glad I couldn't stop laughing all the way back to the shop.

BILLY, aged 9

Bus to school

Rounding a corner
It comes to a stay.
Quick! Grab a rail!
Now we're off on our way . . .
Oh, but it's Thursday,
The day or fear!—
Three hateful lessons!
And school draws near.

Here in the bus though
There's plenty to see:
Boys full of talk about
Last night's T.V.;

Girls with their violins,
Armfuls of twigs
And flowers for teacher;
Bartlett and Biggs;

Conductor who chats with them,
Jokes about cricket;
Machine that flicks out
A white ribbon of ticket . . .
Yes, but it's Thursday,
The day of fear!—
Six hateful lessons!
And school draws near.

Conductor now waiting,
Firm as a rock,
For Billy, whose penny's
Slid down in his sock.
Conductor frowning,
With finger on handle;
Poor Billy blushes,
Undoes his sandal . . .

'Hold very tight, please!
Any more fares?'
Whistling conductor
Goes clumping upstairs . . .
Boots up above now!
Boys coming down! . . .
Over the hump-bridge
And into the town.

Old Warren sweeping
In his shirt-sleeves!
Sun on his shop-front,
Sun on the leaves . . .
Only, it's Thursday,
The day of fear!—
All hateful lessons!
And school draws near.

JOHN WALSH

First dip

Wave after wavelet goes
Coldly over your toes
And sinks down into the stones.
Another mounts to your knees,
Icy, as if to freeze
Flesh and marrow and bones.
And now another, a higher,
Yellow with foam, and dire
With weed from yesterday's storm.
With a gasp you greet it—
Your shoulders stoop to meet it—
And you find . . . you find . . .
   Ah-h-h-h!
You find that the water's warm!

JOHN WALSH

Fishing

I have waited with a long rod
And suddenly pulled a gold-and-greenish, lucent fish from below,
And had him fly like a halo round my head,
Lunging in the air on the line.

Unhooked his gorping, water-horny mouth,
And seen his horror-tilted eye,
His red-gold, water-precious, mirror-flat bright eye;
And felt him beat in my hand, with his mucous, leaping life-throb.

from Fish by D. H. LAWRENCE

Watching

A flock of gulls had come in from the river and were squawking about over the playground looking for bits of bread. It had rained in the night, washing clean the blue paint on the funnel of the concrete ship and giving everything an early morning, fresh-scrubbed look. The bole of the tree had not yet fully dried out. Billandben felt it damp and cold against his bare knees as he clung there, stretched out along the upper fork, straining his eyes across the empty alkali flats for any sign of hostile Comanches.

It was too early for anyone much to be there yet. Some boys from the Peabody Buildings were balancing along the wall at the back, whooping and scuffling, trying to shove each other off. In the playground itself, apart from Billandben, there was just one lone small girl in a yellow hair ribbon. She was riding the rocker, sitting in the front seat and holding on tight, encouraging it first to trot, then canter, then gallop, by drumming against its cast-iron flanks with her heels.

Billandben narrowed his eyes into slits in order to see better what the Peabody gang were up to. Had he thought to bring his Sharp's rifle with him he could have picked them off one by one like crows on a fence rail. But with nothing but his six-shooter he was helpless. There were three, no, four to one. Unless he could get word to the fort to send up reinforcements he had best keep very quiet and lie low.

Except at the Embankment end the great new blocks of yellow brick flats hung over the playground like the walls of an immense gravel pit, eight and nine and even ten storeys high. They had little carpets of grass around them and all the side roads were cobbled. They were called Scott and Dickens and Thackeray and the names of other famous authors. You couldn't see it from the playground, but behind the flats was St. Justin's church, which was why the estate was called St. Justin's Estate. There was a school too, St. Justin's C. of E. Primary, which was built of bricks so black that they looked like coal blocks, and had the date 1882 over its door. Nobody went there much, though, except some of the younger kids from Peabody who lived in the two facing rows of buildings over against the railway.

from *The Latchkey Children* by ERIC ALLEN

Hide and seek

Yoohoo! I'm ready! Come and find me!

The sacks in the toolshed smell like the seaside.
You make yourself little in the salty dark,
Close your eyes tight and hope your feet aren't showing.
Better not risk another call, they might be close.

Don't sneeze whatever happens. The floor is cold.
They're probably searching the bushes near the swing.
What's that? That sounds like them. They're coming in!
Don't breathe or move. Still. Someone knocks a can.
Feet mutter. Somebody comes very close,
A scuffle of words, a laugh, and then they're gone.
They might be back. Careful in case they come.
They'll try the greenhouse, then in here again.
They're taking a long time, but they'll come back.
Risk a peep out, perhaps? Not yet; they might creep in.
A good hiding-place, this: the best you've ever found.
It's funny though, they haven't tried again.
Can't hear a thing. They must be miles away.
The dark damp smell of sand is thicker now.
Give them another call: *Yoo-hoo! Come and find me!*
But they are still elsewhere. They'll think you're clever,
And ask you where you hid. Don't tell them. Keep it secret.
It's cold in here. You can't hear anything.
But wait. Let them hunt a little longer;
Think of them frowning at each other;
Where can he be? We've looked all over.
Something tickles on your nose. Your legs are stiff.
Just a little longer and then creep out.
They're not coming back. You've tricked them properly.
All right. Push off the sacks. That's better.
Good to be rid of that unpleasant smell.
Out of the shed. *Hey! Here I am! I'm here!*
I've won the game! You couldn't find me!
The darkening garden watches. Nothing stirs.
The bushes hold their breath. The air is cold.
Yes, here you are, but where are they who sought you?

VERNON SCANNELL

The two executioners stalk along over the knolls,
Bearing two axes with heavy heads shining and wide,
And a long limp two-handled saw toothed for cutting great
boles,
And so they approach the proud tree that bears the death-mark
on its side.

Jackets doffed they swing axes and chop away just above
ground
And the chips fly about and lie white on the moss and fallen
leaves;
Till a broad deep gash in the bark is hewn all the way round,
And one of them tries to hook upward a rope, which at last he
achieves.

The saw then begins, till the top of the tall giant shivers:
The shivers are seen to grow greater each cut than before:
They edge out the saw, tug the rope; but the tree only quivers,
And kneeling and sawing again, they step back to try pulling once
more.

Then, lastly, the living mast sways, further sways; with a shout
Job and Ike rush aside. Reached the end of its long staying
powers
The tree crashes downward: it shakes all its neighbours throughout
And two hundred year's steady growth has been ended in less
than two hours.

THOMAS HARDY

I wish I were . . .

When the gong sounds at ten in the morning and I walk to school
    by our lane,
Every day I meet the hawker crying, 'Bangles, crystal bangles!'
There is nothing to hurry him on, there is no road he must take,
    no place he must go to, no time when he must come home.
I wish I were a hawker, spending my day in the road, crying,
    'Bangles, crystal bangles!'

When at four in the afternoon I come back from the school,
I can see through the gate of that house the gardener digging the
    ground.
He does what he likes with his spade, he soils his clothes with the
    dust,
Nobody takes him to task if he gets baked in the sun or gets wet.
I wish I were a gardener digging away at the garden with nobody,
    to stop me from digging.

Just as it gets dark in the evening and my mother sends me to
    bed,
I can see through my open window the watchman walking up and
    down.
The lane is dark and lonely, and the street-lamp stands
Like a giant with one red eye in its head.

The watchman swings his lantern and walks with his shadow at
    his side, and never once goes to bed in his life.
I wish I were a watchman walking the streets all night, chasing
    the shadows with my lantern.

RABINDRANATH TAGORE

List of Illustrations

Acknowledgements

The author would like to thank the following publishers, authors and executors for permission to quote from their publications:
George Allen and Unwin Ltd. 'Hot Cake' from *Chinese Poems* translated by Arthur Waley; B. T. Batsford Ltd. *Creative Writing for Juniors* by Barry Maybury; B.B.C. Publications. 'Windy Boy in a Windswept Tree' by Geoffrey Summerfield from *Adventures in English*; Brockhampton Press Ltd. 'Tortoise' by David Speechley from *The Eye of Innocence*; Curtis Brown Ltd. *The Only Child* by James Kirkup; Jonathan Cape Ltd. *The Short Stories of Liam O'Flaherty*; 'Fog' by Carl Sandburg from *Chicago Poems*; Chatto and Windus Ltd. *The Excitement of Writing* edited by A. B. Clegg; 'Winter' from *Confessio Juvenis* by Richard Hughes; The Daily Mirror Newspapers Ltd. *Children as Writers*; J. M. Dent and Sons Ltd. *Under Milk Wood*, *Quite Early One Morning*, *Portrait of the Artist as a Young Dog* by Dylan Thomas; Andre Deutsch Ltd. *The Gravel Ponds* by Peter Levi; Doubleday and Co., Inc. 'Snake' and 'My Papa's Waltz' by Theodore Roethke from *Collected Poems*; 'What is White' by Mary O'Neill from *Hailstones and Halibut Bones*; E. P. Dutton and Co., Inc. 'Jump or Jiggle' from *Another Here and Now Story Book* by Lucy Sprague Mitchell; Faber and Faber Ltd. 'My Papa's Waltz' by Theodore Roethke from *The Collected Poems* of Theodore Roethke; 'An Otter' from *Lupercal* by Ted Hughes; Hugh Finn and International P.E.N. 'Beetle' from *New Poems 1954* (Michael Joseph Ltd.); Harcourt, Brace and World, Inc. 'in Just spring' by e. e. cummings from *Poems 1923–1954*; 'Worms and the Wind' by Carl Sandburg from *Complete Poems*; George G. Harrap and Co. Ltd. 'Autumn' by Florence Hoatson; *The Goalkeeper's Revenge* by Bill Naughton; Rupert Hart-Davis. 'Hard Frost' by Andrew Young from *Collected Poems*; 'The Lonely Farmer' by R. S. Thomas from *Song at the Year's Turning*; *Encounter with Animals* by Gerald Durrell; William Heinemann Ltd. 'Jargon' from *Ragged Robin*, 'Waiting' and 'Beech Leaves' from *Wandering Moon*, 'Slowly' and 'Grey' from *Hurdy Gurdy* by James Reeves; 'Breathless' by Wilfrid Noyce from *South Col*; 'Storm in the Black Forest' and 'Fish' by D. H. Lawrence from *The Complete Poems*; David Higham Associates Ltd. *It Was A Long Time Ago* by Eleanor Farjeon; Hodder and Stoughton Ltd. 'The Summit' by Edmund Hillary from *The Ascent of Everest* by Sir John Hunt; The Hogarth Press Ltd. *Cider with Rosie* by Laurie Lee; Holt, Rinehart and Winston, Inc. 'Fog' by Carl Sandburg from *Chicago Poems*; Hutchinson Publishing Group Ltd. 'Just Old Men' from *Young Writers, Young Readers* edited by Boris Ford; Michael Joseph Ltd. *There is a Happy Land* by Keith Waterhouse; The Literary Trustees of Walter de la Mare and The Society of Authors as their representative. 'An Abandoned Church' by Walter de la Mare; MacGibbon and Kee. 'in Just spring' by e. e. cummings from *Complete Poems*, 'Through the Tunnel' from *The Habit of Loving* by Doris Lessing; 'The Term' and 'This is just to say' by William Carlos Williams from *The Collected Earlier Poems*; Methuen and Co. Ltd. 'Smells' by C. Morley from *Chimney Smoke*; Mrs. D. M. Mewton-Wood. 'India' by W. J. Turner from *The Hunter*; New Directions Publishing Corporation. 'The Term' and 'This is Just to Say' by William Carlos Williams; Novello and Co. Ltd. *The Wind Wafts Little Creatures* by Kevin Crossely-Holland; Oxford University Press. *The Latchkey Children* by Eric Allen; Penguin Books Ltd. 'Sink Song' by J. A. Lindon from *Yet More Comic and Curious Verse*; 'The Fish' by W. W. E. Ross from *The Penguin Book of Canadian Verse*; various extracts from *Miracles* edited by Richard Lewis; A. D. Peters. *The End of the Road* by Hilaire Belloc; Michell Raper. 'Morning Glory'; Routledge and Kegan Paul Ltd. *Poems by Children* edited by Michael Baldwin; Simon and Schuster Inc. various extracts from *Miracles*; Myfanwy Thomas for 'After Tain' and 'Tall Nettles' by Edward Thomas; Trustees for the Copyrights of the late Dylan Thomas; A. P. Watt and Son. 'To a Squirrel at Kyle-na-no' from *Collected Poems of W. B. Yeats*; and Gareth Owen, Geoffrey Summerfield, and the staff and children of Churchfields School, West Bromwich, Coombe Country Girls' School, New Malden, the Grove C.P., Malvern, St. John's C.P., Kidderminster, and Stourport C.P. schools for permission to reproduce their own work.

Author Index